Christian
Tolerance

Biblical Perspectives on Current Issues
HOWARD CLARK KEE, General Editor

CHARISMATA: God's Gifts for God's People
 by John Koenig   ISBN 0-664-24176-X

THE COMMITTED MARRIAGE
 by Elizabeth Achtemeier   ISBN 0-664-24754-7

DIALOGUE: The Key to Understanding Other Religions
 by Donald K. Swearer   ISBN 0-664-24138-7

HOW GOD DEALS WITH EVIL
 by W. Sibley Towner   ISBN 0-664-24127-1

THE INSPIRATION OF SCRIPTURE: Problems and Proposals
 by Paul J. Achtemeier   ISBN 0-664-24313-4

IS CHRIST THE END OF THE LAW?
 by Gerard S. Sloyan   ISBN 0-664-24190-5

IS THERE HOPE FOR THE CITY?
 by Donald W. Shriver, Jr., and Karl A. Ostrom   ISBN 0-664-24147-6

THE PREDICAMENT OF THE PROSPEROUS
 by Bruce C. Birch and Larry L. Rasmussen ISBN 0-664-24211-1

CHRISTIAN TOLERANCE: Paul's Message to the Modern Church
 by Robert Jewett   ISBN 0-664-24444-0

Christian Tolerance

PAUL'S MESSAGE
TO THE MODERN CHURCH

ROBERT JEWETT

THE WESTMINSTER PRESS

PHILADELPHIA

First edition

Published by The Westminster Press®
Philadelphia, Pennsylvania

PRINTED IN THE UNITED STATES OF AMERICA
1 2 3 4 5 6 7 8 9

Library of Congress Cataloging in Publication Data

Jewett, Robert.
  Christian tolerance.

  (Biblical perspectives on current issues)
  Includes index.
  1. Religious tolerance—Biblical teaching.
2. Bible. N.T. Epistles of Paul—Criticism, interpretation, etc. I. Title. II. Series.
BS2655.R33J48 1982   280'.042   82-13480
ISBN 0-664-24444-0 (pbk.)

CONTENTS

EDITOR'S PREFACE

There was a day when Christian piety was largely a private matter. Now, in the last quarter of the twentieth century, that is scarcely possible. In the name of Christ, powerful efforts are under way to unseat politicians, to gain support for religious convictions and values, to force major denominations in certain political or doctrinal directions. Others seek to combat these undertakings—also in the name of Christ. Still others, in the name of ecumenism, continue to work quietly at uniting all Christians around a common center of conviction and acceptance. Yet dramatic changes in church participation—including a decline of membership in major denominations and a surge of support for evangelical enterprises—call into question both the wisdom and the potential effectiveness of the three-decade-long ecumenical search for common ground as a base for Christian peace and unity.

In such a time and circumstance, Robert Jewett's perceptive analytical study of tolerance and of fundamental disagreements within the churches of Paul—and specifically, the church at Rome—is profoundly relevant and needed. He shows that the first generation of Christians, though united in the conviction that in Christ God was reconciling the world to himself (II Cor. 5:19), were in serious disagreement over matters of admission to the church, standards of Christian behavior, attitudes toward Jewish law and Roman culture. It is in such a situation of profound differences and resulting conflict that Paul urges Christians to "welcome one another." Dr. Jewett's combined gifts of scholarly analysis and sensitivity to the current scene unite effectively in this book to address the conflict situations that divide the church today, and it points the way to constructive peace that does not disguise profound differences, but prevents disagreement from dividing Christ's People.

HOWARD CLARK KEE

THE DILEMMA OF TOLERANCE TODAY

In the fall of 1981 there was a small-scale book burning sponsored by a group called "The Immoral Minority" that symbolizes the dilemma of tolerance. A group of university students invited reporters and photographers to view their burning of fundamentalist Christian pamphlets in protest of the "religious repressionism being demonstrated by today's Christian power bloc." The students were particularly upset by recent burnings of secular books and rock albums sponsored by religious groups. "A small number of Christian fundamentalist groups are wanting to burn ideas and thoughts that have no reason to be burned," said the leader of the student group as he threw pamphlets into the fire. As one of the members explained, "the group does not endorse such burnings . . . and only did it to show how wrong it is."[1] It was a rather incongruous episode, but perhaps no more so than dozens of other book burnings that have been reported around the country in recent months. It confirms the appropriateness of Martin E. Marty's reply to the question about the key problem American religion is now facing. "The problem is that the civil people are not committed and the committed people aren't civil," he told a *Chicago Tribune* religion editor.[2] Those who are in favor of the tradition of tolerance and the free expression of ideas seem to lack internal support for their convictions, while many who hold passionate religious convictions feel compelled to repudiate the tradition of tolerance itself.

The decline in tolerance is not confined to the church and the political sphere. University audiences routinely shout down speakers whose views they disapprove. Spokespersons of the right as well as the left decry the exercise of free expression of ideas by their adversaries. Leading scholars such as Robert Paul Wolff and Herbert Marcuse have argued that tolerance is repressive because it allows evil to stand.[3] John Murray Cuddihy has contended that tolerance is nothing more than a polite acknowledgment of our inability to convert the erroneous, a sign of the lack of religious depth of contemporary religionists.[4] In the words of the editors of *Soundings,* introducing a series of articles devoted to this dilemma, "The invisible consensus that once permitted pluralism to be such an attractive idea to Americans has visibly broken apart."[5] One of the articles in the volume, written by Robert Bellah, calls for "the creation of a theology of religious pluralism" to cope with the current vacuum.[6] He shares the assessment of Martin Marty that "the theological program" for this kind of tolerance "is only beginning to be worked out."[7]

I believe that Paul's approach to the problems of pluralism in the epistle to the Romans offers a decisive resource for reformulating a doctrine of tolerance on specifically Christian grounds. Although Paul's contribution has been alluded to by scholars such as Ernst Käsemann and Hans-Werner Bartsch,[8] it has never played a role in the discussion of tolerance in North America. For reasons that I will detail in Chapter I, Paul remains an unacknowledged ally in the quest for the foundations of a tolerant society. My plan is to concentrate on the material from Paul's letter to the Romans, showing the relation between the ethic of mutual tolerance and the problems of conscience, mission, congregational relations, and the setting of limits. Since I am in the early stages of research and reflection in preparation for writing a formal commentary on Romans, much of what I write here is necessarily preliminary. My hope is to

wrench Romans out of the hands of the enemies of tolerance who have dominated our interpretation for so long and
to suggest the relevance of Pauline thought for our current
dilemma. Above all, I feel bound to follow Paul's conten-
tion, even against my own personal prejudices, that tolerance in the Christian community is not a liberal doctrine. It
encompasses both conservative and liberal theological systems, whether in the early church or in the current situation. To state the thesis in advance: Tolerance is the
expression of authentic faith in the God who transcends
race and creed, but who calls conservatives and liberals,
Jews and Greeks, men and women into the service of
righteousness.

Chapter I

STRENUOUS TOLERANCE FLOWING FROM VITAL FAITH

To develop a Biblical theory of tolerance and to reflect on its embodiment in the cultural traditions shaped by the Bible may seem to be an overly audacious task. For the widespread consensus is that the Bible looms as the deadly enemy of tolerance. One of the international authorities in the history of religions has recently surveyed the evidence that led earlier scholars to conclude that the victory of Christianity was due to the fact that it was more intolerant than any other religion or philosophy in the ancient world. Carl Schneider concedes that there are grounds for intolerance in the Old Testament that early Christians took over from Judaism, but contends that the major factor was the influence of Paul. Paul's letter to the Galatians is, in his view, "an explicit document of religious intolerance" in which Paul utters the "anathema, . . . the strongest term for a total accursedness."[1] Although the process of banning heretics had previously been developed in Jewish synagogues, it was an innovation for Paul to utter the curse on his own authority alone. Paul's mystical identification of himself with Christ produced radical intolerance, in Schneider's view, because Paul thereby placed himself in the judgment seat of God. He concludes that "intolerance belongs not to the essence of Christianity but to the essence of Paul."[2]

Although the traditional interpretation of Paul sustains

Schneider's conclusion, I would like to show that recent advances in our understanding of the Pauline letters and the situations in his churches require a radical revision of this view. Paul is in fact an advocate of an active form of tolerance. His long-term commitment to coexistence and fellowship between competing groups in the early church, particularly between Jewish Christians and Gentile Christians, is visible in every letter. What has been taken as intolerance in Galatians, I would argue, is in fact a repudiation of the intolerant campaign of Judaizers who rejected coexistence with Gentiles and demanded incorporation of all church members, regardless of their racial background and theological outlook, into Judaism. In Paul's letter to the Romans, the most influential theological writing in early Christianity, there is a systematic argument in favor of tolerantly accepting competing groups within the church. In this chapter, I would like to analyze a key statement of this tolerant ethic in Rom. 15:7: "Welcome one another, therefore, as Christ has welcomed you, for the glory of God." Before we turn to this material in Romans, however, there is a question to be answered: If the argument of Romans points in the direction of tolerance, why has this not been widely seen before?

I

There are several decisive reasons why Paul's contribution to the theory and practice of tolerance has been largely overlooked or misunderstood. The first of these is touched on by Hans-Werner Bartsch in an article on the idea of tolerance in Paul.[3] Ever since the times of Marcion and Augustine, Christian controversialists have found the antitheses in Pauline thought very appealing. Galatians in particular has been influential in this regard, with its distinctions between a true and a false gospel, a religion of law and circumcision versus a religion of grace and freedom, the old age versus the new. The Lutheran antithesis between law and gospel, with its correlate of Catholic versus Protestant approaches to salvation, is derived from this source. It played a crucial role in Ferdinand Christian Baur's influential nineteenth-century account of the history of early Christian thought in which Paul was placed in polar opposition to Judaism: a particularistic religion of law posed against a universalistic religion of grace, marking a decisive alternative in religion that runs through every successive age. Although the legacy of Baur has been substantially repudiated by New Testament scholars, argues Bartsch, the influence of this idea of polarity is abiding. It encouraged the development of anti-Semitism, which was precisely the opposite effect from that which Paul intended to achieve in his most extensive discussion of the issues, Romans 9–11.

The second reason for overlooking the potential contribution of Paul in favor of tolerant pluralism is the long-standing problem in understanding the role of authority in first-generation Christianity. Paul introduces himself in Galatians as "Paul an apostle—not from men nor through man, but through Jesus Christ and God the Father." Interpreters of these words have traditionally understood Paul's authority in terms of legitimacy, that is, as a fully institutionalized official with unlimited powers. Therefore Paul's statement a few verses later, "If any one is preaching to you a gospel contrary to that which you received, let him be accursed" (Gal. 1:9), was generally taken to mean that Paul was speaking as an agent, capable of making the excommunication stick simply because of his official standing. This view has been challenged by studies written recently by John Howard Schütz and Bengt Holmberg.[4]

Using distinctions from Max Weber, Schütz has clarified the confusion between official legitimacy and charismatic authority, showing that Paul had the latter but not the former. This explains why he was in a position to urge strongly that a local congregation should take a certain action, but was willing to allow that congregation to come to its own decision and make the final judgment. The assumption, after all, was that they too were charismatics, endued by the powers of the new age, and thus called upon by God to make local decisions in the light of their own judgment. This explains why Paul was able to demand the expulsion, for incestuous conduct, of a prominent church member in I Cor. 5:2–13 but to acquiesce in II Cor. 2:5–11 when the church evidently came to another decision in a similar instance. The radical equality expressed in the well-known summary, "There is neither Jew nor Greek, there is neither slave nor free, there is neither male nor female; for you are all one in Christ Jesus" (Gal. 3:28), is thus consistent with the charismatic authority that he shared, in one form or another, with every member of the new community. The problem was that succeeding generations did not share the charismatic experience of radical grace and equality; they were inclined to understand Paul's authority in terms of legitimacy. What was intended as a series of strongly worded arguments from one charismatic to other charismatics was thus transformed into the legally binding judgment of an official whose powers were institutionally sanctioned and thus irrefutable. If Paul possessed such official powers and made such sweeping pronouncements, it followed that later Christian leaders should have similar prerogatives and should carry them out in a consistent manner. One can trace the first stages of this process in the work of the Pauline school, the group responsible for the editing of the Pauline letters and the creation of the pastoral epistles, both of which had decisive influence on the rise of official intolerance among Christian leaders.

This leads directly to a consideration of the third reason for misunderstanding Paul's views about tolerance. Not until the rise of the historical-critical method of interpretation was it possible to separate the genuine from the spurious Pauline letters or to detect the occasional interpolations in the genuine letters. Earlier generations of the church simply assumed that it was really Paul who vicious-

ly stereotyped opposing church leaders as "rejecting conscience" (I Tim. 1:19) and who taught that, because "their
talk will eat its way like gangrene" (II Tim. 2:17), such
persons must be excommunicated (I Tim. 1:20) and hence-
forth strictly avoided (II Tim. 3:5), and that if they are still
inside the congregation, their freedom of speech must be
revoked (Titus 1:11). Although critical scholars are now
generally agreed that the intolerant views in these "pastoral
epistles" are vastly different from Paul's, the tendency
remains to tar the authentic letters with the same brush.
Read in the light of I and II Timothy and Titus, many
statements in the authentic letters appeared and still appear
to be narrow-minded, authoritarian, and highly bigoted.

The fact that there are several interpolations in the
genuine letters deriving from the same hands that wrote I
and II Timothy and Titus makes the matter more difficult to
disentangle. Several years ago I set forth in detail the
evidence concerning such interpolations in the Corinthian
correspondence, including phrases like "This is my rule in
all the churches" (I Cor. 4:17; 7:17; 11:16) which imply that
Paul arbitrarily imposed a uniform ethic of Judaic origin on
all his churches.[5] The same intolerant perspective is visible
in the "Let women be silent" passage in I Cor. 14:33b–36,
which has been identified as an interpolation on the basis
of its disparities with the context, its contradictions to the
rest of I Corinthians, and its non-Pauline vocabulary.[6]

Perhaps the most significant of these interpolations from
the perspective of the tolerance question is that found in
Romans 16:

> [17]I appeal to you, brethren, to look out for those who create
> dissensions and scandals, in opposition to the doctrine
> which you have been taught; avoid them. [18]For such persons
> do not serve our Lord Christ, but their own bellies, and by
> fair and flattering words they deceive the hearts of the
> simple-minded. [19]For while your obedience is known to all,
> so that I rejoice over you, I would have you wise as to what
> is good and guileless as to what is evil; [20]then the God

of peace will soon crush Satan under your feet. (Rom. 16:17–20)

The definitive case for identifying this as an antignostic polemic not originally intended for Rome was made by Walter Schmithals.[7] John Knox has noted the disparities between these verses and the rest of Romans and concludes that they would be "accounted for with least difficulty when thought of as reflecting the situation in the period of the Pastoral and the Catholic epistles, i.e., in the first half of the second century."[8]

A description of the intolerant motifs in Rom. 16:17–20 in the context of their contradictions with genuine Pauline material will serve to focus the issue:

The verb translated "look out for" in Rom. 16:17 is never used with this peculiar sense of "avoid" in the other Pauline letters.[9] The conclusion of this verse contains an even stronger exclusionary sense: "avoid them," an expression never used in Pauline exhortation about dealings with fellow Christians. The closest parallels are in the pastoral epistles (II Tim. 3:5; Titus 3:9–10), while in the authentic portions of Romans the very opposite admonition is developed: "As for the man who is weak in faith, welcome him, but not for disputes over opinions" (Rom. 14:1; cf. 15:7). This has an obvious bearing on how Christians are to deal with ideological opponents within their communities. The intolerant implications of Rom. 16:17 are followed in churches such as the Lutheran Church—Missouri Synod which refuse to share pulpit and altar with other Christians.[10]

The basis of intolerant exclusion in Rom. 16:17 is "dissensions and scandals, in opposition to the doctrine which you have been taught," which implies that disputation itself is heresy and that anyone questioning tradition is subject to this charge. The opposite view is developed in Rom. 14:1 to 15:13, where conservatives and liberals are admonished to remain true to their doctrinal convictions and their varying liturgical practices while accepting one another as brothers and sisters in Christ. The use of the term *didachē* in the sense of "doctrine" to which one must subscribe to be a legitimate Christian differs from its use in the other authentic Pauline letters (Rom. 6:17; I Cor. 14:6, 26) but is consistent with its use in the pastorals (II Tim. 4:2; Titus 1:9). This passage has thus provided a crucial basis for heresy proceedings against nonconformists whose stubborn maintenance of their integrity causes "dissension." One could virtually write the history of the hounding of nonconformists in Massachusetts Bay Colony under the rubric of this verse.

The *ad hominem* argument in Rom. 16:18 is unparalleled in the authentic Pauline letters because it lacks theological grounding. The expression "serving their own bellies" appears to be adapted from the antilibertine polemic in Phil. 3:19, where it was linked with an explicit reference to enmity to the cross of Christ on grounds of a radical doctrine of freedom from moral limitations.[11] Here it serves simply to smear and discredit opponents by calling their motivations into question. The expression "fair and flattering words" is a stereotypical depiction of intellectual speech whose closest parallels are I Tim. 1:7 and II Tim. 2:14 as well as the interpolation in I Cor. 11:16. The very gifts of rhetorical excellence that Paul develops to a fine art in Romans and his other letters, as recent research has proven, are here classified as heretical. Whereas Paul warns the "strong" in Rom. 14:13–21 and I Cor. 8:9–12 not to use their superior knowledge and argumentative ability in such a way as to impair the integrity of others, Rom. 16:18 in effect disqualifies such intellectual gifts in the life of the church. This verse contains the patronizing assumption that the "simple-minded" cannot defend themselves against such intellectual powers, which is the opposite of the assumption that one draws from Rom. 14:3–16, where the "weak" are depicted as self-righteous bigots engaged in "judging" the intellectual liberals for not living up to the

proper standards. As Käsemann rather caustically recasts
the thought of this verse, it boils down to "the exploitation
of poor believers by sinful gluttons."[12] Again, one could
write chapters in the history of the harassment and discrediting of intellectuals by ecclesiastical authorities under the
banner of this vicious verse.

Romans 16:19 demands "obedience" in an absolute
sense unparalleled elsewhere in Romans but rather close to
II Cor. 7:15 and 10:5, 6. It is one thing to speak of
"obedience" to the apostle who founded the Corinthian
church, which was directly related to the gospel to which
Paul was himself obedient. But it is quite another thing to
speak of the "obedience" of the Romans whom Paul had
never met. This formulation counters the care with which
Paul designates his relation to the Roman Christians as
"mutual strengthening by each other's faith" (Rom. 1:12) on
the premise that "you yourselves are full of goodness, filled
with all knowledge, and able to instruct one another" (Rom.
15:14). Elsewhere in Romans as well as in the other
authentic letters, Paul correlates "obedience" with "faith"
and "gospel," making it clear that it is one's response to
God's powerful message of grace that defines obedience.
But in v. 19 we find the doctrine of obedience that became
popular in the era of "Early Catholicism," in which submission to authoritative leaders and their teachings became the
essence of faith (cf. I Tim. 4:11 to 6:21; II Tim. 1:13 to 3:17;
Titus 2:1–10).

The doctrine of obedience in Rom. 16:19 is linked with
being "wise as to what is good and guileless as to what is
evil" in a way that flatly contradicts Paul's earlier argument
in Romans. In this verse the discernment of good and evil is
simply a matter of obeying authority; to be obedient is to do
the "good," no matter what the content of the command;
obedience retains guilelessness or innocence because the
obedient break no rules. Paul ruled out such innocence on
principle with his extensive argument from Rom 1:18 to
3:20 that all persons, Gentiles and Jews alike, sin and lose

their innocence through idolatry or pride. Obedience to the rules in particular is counterproductive, he argues, "for no human being will be justified in God's sight by works of the law" (Rom. 3:20). But those who receive the gospel of the grace of God enter into a process of transformation in which they exercise their own judgment about what is "good." The admonition of Rom. 12:2 is to avoid mere conformity to the will of others: "Do not be conformed to this world but be transformed by the renewal of your mind, that you may prove what is the will of God, what is good and acceptable and perfect." This doctrine of moral autonomy, in which each Christian examines for himself or herself how to fulfill the law of love (Rom. 13:8), is completely eliminated by the authoritarian command of Rom. 16:19. The path is thereby opened to the "holy obedience" demanded by Ignatius Loyola, which consists of submitting to "whatever may be enjoined on us with readiness . . . by persuading ourselves that all things [commanded] are just; by rejecting with a kind of blind obedience all opposing opinion or judgements of our own."[13] If obedience to authority is the sole test of good and evil, the possibility of tolerance is logically excluded and the rationale for persecuting dissenters is rendered invincible.

The blessing formula of Rom. 16:20 lacks the subtle verbal form of all the other Pauline blessings that begin, "Now may the God of peace bless you . . . " Its content is also vastly different from the other blessings that I have studied.[14] That God brings peace by "crushing Satan under your feet" as you obediently repress heretics is precisely the antithesis of Paul's earlier argument in Romans. The "weak" and the "strong" are urged in 14:1 to 15:13 to cease the effort to repress and convert one another. The destructive stereotype that their opponents were satanic, leading to their "judging" and "despising" one another, was replaced by the idea that one's opponents are the "householders" of God whose obligation is to conform to his will rather than to each other (14:4–12). Romans 16:20 encourages factions within the church to disregard Paul's previous argument, to view their opponents not as conscientious servants of the same God but rather as demonic agents. Whereas the blessings in the authentic section (Rom. 15:5–6, 13) extol the promise of coexistence between ideological opponents, this blessing guarantees total victory with the apocalyptic image of smashing God's enemies under one's feet at the moment of the final battle.[15] This is a verse with a fateful legacy, cited repeatedly in the condemnation of heretics and the burning of witches throughout the course of Christian history. It is the dreadful capstone of the most influential single passage in the tradition of Christian intolerance. With these non-Pauline verses standing at the climactic end of the epistle to the Romans, there was little opportunity for earlier generations to detect the actual views of the apostle in favor of tolerance.

In the light of these details, the fourth reason that Paul's doctrine of tolerance has had so little effect can be quickly stated. Whereas Paul's most extensive statement of the idea of tolerant pluralism in the church is in Romans, that letter was so consistently cited by the enemies of tolerance that Paul's actual views could scarcely surface. When one considers two of the principal traditions of tolerance in Western culture, the one deriving from the Renaissance and forming a line from Erasmus through Bodin, Castellio, and Grotius to John Locke, and the other deriving from the left wing of the Reformation and articulated in the work of persons like Schwenkfeld, Franck, Milton, and Roger Williams, it is striking that Romans so rarely provided the basis for advocating liberty. The material in Romans 16 was constantly used by supporters of repression, and the opening verses in Romans 13 provided an argument for submission to governmental authority in every circumstance:

> Let every person be subject to the governing authorities. For there is no authority except from God, and those that exist have been instituted by God. Therefore he who resists the

authorities resists what God has appointed, and those who
resist will incur judgment. . . . But if you do wrong, be afraid,
for he does not bear the sword in vain; he is the servant of
God to execute his wrath on the wrongdoer. Therefore one
must be subject, not only to avoid God's wrath but also for
the sake of conscience. (Rom. 13:1–5)

These verses inspired Luther's conservative support of the
sword of the state against unruly peasants and heretics.
They were cited by Calvinists as well as by Roman Catholics in support of legal prosecution and punishment of
dissenters and counter religionists. In the British and
American settings during Colonial times, this passage provided support for royalists who resisted the exercise of
liberty. The consequence was that when advocates of
tolerance sought New Testament backing for their views,
their resources were Galatians, I and II Corinthians, and
the Gospels, not Romans. The most significant single argument in favor of tolerance that was available in the entirety
of Scripture, in Rom. 14:1 to 15:13, was therefore a casualty
of the partisan struggles within Christendom. Its relevance
was so obfuscated by the antiheretical interpolation in
16:17–20 and so limited by the traditional interpretation of
13:1–7 that it could not surface to provide the positive
rationale for tolerance that it clearly contained.

II

In order to grasp the significance of the verse in Romans
that encapsulates the doctrine of tolerance flowing from
vital faith (15:7), there is required a sense of how it fits into
the argument of the letter and the historical situation that
the letter addressed. This literary and historical perspective
may help to overcome the legacy of misunderstanding
Romans. There is a general consensus among current exegetes that 14:1 to 15:13 is a kind of "special exhortation" to
the "strong" and the "weak" parties in the Roman church.[16]
Wilhelm Wuellner has recently called this section an *exem-*

plum in which the practical results of the theological argumentation are "concretized."[17] There are disagreements about the precise identification of these parties or tendencies, but most would agree that these two chapters develop what Ernest Findlay Scott called "the great principle of individual liberty."[18] Here Paul advocates "mutual tolerance" between the factions in the Roman church on grounds of maintaining personal integrity and seeking harmony in the church.[19] Within the scope of this argument, Rom. 15:7 functions as a kind of recapitulation in exhortative form:

> Welcome one another
> as Christ has welcomed you
> for the glory of God.

Its relation to the rest of the argument may be clarified by a brief analysis. Romans 14:1–9 sets forth the theological basis for mutual acceptance between the weak and the strong in Rome. The next three verses show why one should avoid violating this principle of mutual acceptance, and vs. 13–23 advise the avoidance of "stumbling blocks" and "revulsions." Romans 15:1–13 urges the readers to glorify God by complying with this ethic of mutual acceptance. It begins with admonitions to the weak and the strong (15:1–2) which are sustained by theological justification (15:2–4) and blessed with a benediction (15:5–6). Our crucial verse (15:7) opens the subsection that admonishes the Romans to act so as to demonstrate the hope of the Gentile mission. It recapitulates the ethic of mutual acceptance whose effect will be to show how both Jews and Gentiles come in the gospel to praise God, thus fulfilling their destiny and confirming the promises made to Israel that all peoples will unite under God's rule.

The question of the historical setting for this admonition to mutual tolerance has been deeply entangled for a long time with the puzzling purpose and genre of Romans. It is different from the other Pauline letters in that it is not addressed to a church that Paul himself has founded. The fact that it contains such extensive theological argumentation and appears to be rather vaguely related to a concrete congregational situation has led scholars, including myself at an earlier stage of my study, to conclude that Romans was a kind of theological treatise, or in W. G. Kümmel's words, "the theological self-confession of Paul."[20] The collection of essays edited by Karl Paul Donfried has served to clarify this issue, and in particular, Wilhelm Wuellner's identification of the literary genre has helped me to grasp the differences between Romans and the other letters.[21] Whereas the latter fit into the forensic/apologetic or the deliberative genres of classical Greco-Roman rhetoric, Romans appears to conform more closely to the demonstrative genre. To be more precise, I would argue that Romans fits one of the subtypes in the demonstrative genre, the "Ambassadorial Letter," and that the formal features in the opening, the closing, and the development of the argument as well as the diplomatic vagueness of the situational details fit the distinctive purpose for which this letter was intended.[22] Paul in fact intends to visit Rome on his way to Spain, and he desires support and contacts to open his mission there. In order to gain this support, he must clarify the nature of the gospel to be preached and overcome the hostilities between factions in the Roman house churches pertaining to the status of Jews and Gentiles in the plan of salvation. The argument about tolerance in chs. 14 and 15 thus serves as a climax of the theological argumentation of Romans, exemplifying what the gospel of the grace of God achieves in the face of hostile divisions.

It is therefore possible, in view of these recent developments, to agree with Karl Donfried that "any study of Romans should proceed on the initial assumption that this letter was written by Paul to deal with a concrete situation in Rome,"[23] that ch. 16 was originally intended to address the same audience,[24] and that the entire letter aims at eliciting support for Paul's controversial mission to the

Gentiles as far west as Spain. The ethic of the final two
chapters is thus integral to the purpose of Romans, and 15:7
is one of several verses that sum up the essence of the
entire argument. In other words, the tolerant ethic is
integral to the message of the letter about the "gospel of
Jesus Christ."

It is crucial to grasp the background of the admonition,
"Welcome one another," in Rom. 15:7. The situation of the
Jewish community in Rome and the facts concerning the
early history of the Christian congregations there have been
fairly well known for a long time. Recent archaeological
discoveries concerning the status and size of the Jewish
synagogues in Rome have added to this picture.[25] But these
details could never previously be fitted coherently into the
purpose and genre of Romans, with the result that the
significance of the climactic argument about accepting one
another remained unclear. By moving past the untenable
alternative views of Romans—as an abstract theological
treatise, unrelated to any specific congregational situation,
or as a situational letter like I Corinthians, where Paul
addresses a congregation he has founded and answers
questions its members have directly posed to him—it is
possible to see why Paul speaks to the situation as he does.
He obviously knows a large number of people in Rome by
name, greeting them along with at least five separate house
churches in ch. 16.[26] It is because he knows the situation so
well that he addresses it so carefully. The formality and
vagueness of reference in the identification of the "weak"
and the "strong" which have been the despair of earlier
interpreters fit his ambassadorial purpose exactly. Once
this purpose is clear, some precise implications of "welcome" in view of the recent experience of the Roman
church become clear.[27]

Wolfgang Wiefel has recently assembled the evidence
concerning the origin and development of the Roman
house churches.[28] They had begun in several of the small,
Greek-speaking synagogues in Rome. Since the Jews in

Rome lacked a coherent organization, these synagogues provided a natural seedbed for various kinds of Christian missionizing. "The multitude of congregations, their democratic constitutions, and the absence of a central Jewish governing board made it easy for the missionaries of the new faith to talk in the synagogues and to win new supporters. . . . However, since Rome had no supervising body which could forbid any form of Christian propaganda in the city, it was possible to missionize in various synagogues concurrently or to go successively from one to the other. It is likely that the existence of newly converted Christians alongside the traditional members of the synagogue may have led to increased factions and even to tumultuous disputes."[29]

It was in A.D. 49, some seven or eight years before Paul dictated the letter to the Romans, that a decisive event occurred to form the immediate background of the problem in the house churches that Paul addresses with the admonition to "welcome one another." Riots broke out in the Jewish synagogues, apparently involving Jewish Christian agitators and their zealous Jewish opponents. "Since there was no central Jewish authority to mediate the dispute," Wiefel argues, the emperor "Claudius turned vigorously against all Jews."[30] A large number of Jewish and Christian leaders were expelled from Rome and, according to Dio Cassius, the Jews lost their right to assemble. This meant that the Christians remaining in Rome were almost exclusively Gentile in origin, and that during this period before the Jewish synagogues could open again during the reign of Nero, the Christians would have had to form separate congregations without any ties to the synagogues from which they had sprung. For a five-year period, from A.D. 49 until 54 when Nero came to power with a much friendlier attitude toward the Jews, these Gentile-Christian congregations developed in their own directions. New leaders arose from Latin and Greek quarters of the community, and it seems clear from the details in the argument of Romans that some of them were committed to a radically Pauline form of the faith. Some of them were proud of their freedom from the Jewish law and customs, perhaps even to the point of preferring libertinism. If they were typical of other Greek-speaking Christians of the first generation, many of them would have had charismatic views of the ministry and a liberal outlook on ethical questions. To adapt a term suggested by Paul Minear's reconstruction of the congregational situation, some of these new leaders were "radical emancipationists" who "relished this exhilarating postreligious liberty . . . and favored ridicule and heated debates" with the less enlightened as a "necessary form of therapy."[31]

When the original Jewish-Christian leaders like Prisca and Aquila began to return to Rome in the early years of Nero's reign, they found a changed and threatening situation in the churches they had helped to found. Not only were new leaders in charge, but many of the older, conservative patterns of life and worship that had been carried over from the Jewish synagogues were now altered. Moreover, the long-smoldering anti-Semitic tendencies of the Roman citizenry were becoming pronounced as struggles for congregational leadership ensued.[32] Bartsch, Harder, and others who closely analyzed Romans 9–11 had suspected such tendencies on the part of Gentile Christians, and the reconstruction by Wiefel provides confirmation.[33] In the two years immediately prior to Paul's writing his letter to the Romans, these conflicts between Jewish and Gentile Christians, between liberals and conservatives, between old and new Christians, grew and festered. The controversies undoubtedly crossed racial lines, because there were Jewish Christians who inclined toward the Pauline view of freedom from the law and others who were loyal to the more conservative pattern of Peter and the Jerusalem "mother church." Among the generally liberal Gentiles, there were probably some of a conservative stripe, very likely associated with the two house churches within Roman bureaucracies, "those belonging to Aristobulus" (Rom. 16:10) and "those belonging to Narcissus" (16:11).[34] It is within this tangled situation that the letter to the Romans must be placed. To use the words of Wiefel once again: "It was written to assist the Gentile Christian majority, who are the primary addressees of the letter, to live together with the Jewish Christians in one congregation, thereby putting an end to their quarrels about status."[35]

III

To "welcome one another" (Rom. 15:7) in this context was to accept others into full fellowship, to put an end to the hostile competition, and to admit the basic legitimacy of the other sides. It is clear that this verse is addressed to both the "weak" and the "strong," picking up the admonition from the opening verse in this section (14:1). Ernest Best states the implication in rather general terms: "Let them *accept* (cf. 14:1, 3) each other into the full fellowship of all that goes on in the church as *Christ accepted them.*"[36] But in view of the historical background, it was not so much the question of allowing others a voice in church affairs as of accepting them as legitimate members of the group. The catchwords "weak" and "strong" that Paul employs in the preceding discussion are clearly in view here. They are highly misleading in their modern connotation, implying that the distinction had to do with weakness or strength of convictions and will power. Actually, as the research on this issue has made plain,[37] the terms had probably been imposed by the "strong" who identified their superiority in terms of spiritual courage to defy traditional scruples. Rather than supposing that the "strong" comprised a single group, we may appropriately think of this term as roughly equivalent with "liberal" in the modern political sense, depicting a fairly wide range of ideological, racial, and temperamental differences. Similarly the "weak" should be thought of as roughly equivalent with "conservative," consisting of various groups of Jewish and Gentile Christians favoring a scrupulous attitude toward the Jewish law and certain liturgical and ascetic practices. Some of them apparently retained vegetarian preferences from their Orphic, Pythagorean, or Gnostic backgrounds, but the description makes it plain that they were anything but weak in their convictions. In contrast to a group with the same appellation (the "weak" in I Corinthians), the group in Rome appears to have contained self-righteous bigots who condemned the liberals for not living up to ascetic standards.

Rather than taking up the ideological and racial tensions in precise detail as he does in other letters, Paul seeks to find common ground by developing general principles in a manner consistent with the diplomatic purpose of Romans. Discussions that scholars have taken as exasperatingly vague references to the congregational situation—when one compares Romans with other Pauline letters—are actually part of the genius of Romans. Paul begins with what seems to be an individual case of "the man who is weak in faith" in 14:1 and extends it, by the time he reaches our key verse in 15:7, into a general principle of mutual tolerance. This movement, from an abstract instance to a widely applicable principle, is visible in the opening verses of ch. 14:

> As for the man who is weak in faith, welcome him, but not for disputes over opinions. One believes he may eat anything, while the weak man eats only vegetables. Let not him who eats despise him who abstains, and let not him who abstains pass judgment on him who eats; for God has welcomed him. (Rom. 14:1–3)

It is clear from the wording of these verses that Paul selected the extreme positions on opposite ends of the liberal-conservative spectrum in Rome, with the absolute vegetarian on one end and the complete libertarian on the other, in order to make the principle of tolerance inclusive of all the positions inside this range. The admonition to refrain from despising or judging these extreme positions has the effect of legitimating the fiercely advocated positions along the entire scale of possibilities. The basis of this theory of mutual acceptance is succinctly stated at the end of 14:3: If God accepts my competitors,[38] the person or group against which I am discriminating because of differences of life-style, then who am I to refuse the admonition to "welcome" them as legitimate members of my group?

The same style of argument is visible in the related controversy concerning special days. Once again Paul describes two individuals whose behavior placed them at opposite ends of a spectrum:

> One man esteems one day over another, while another man esteems all days alike. Let every one be fully convinced in his own mind. The one who sets his mind on the day does so in relation to the Lord. He also who eats, eats in relation to the Lord, since he gives thanks to God; while he who abstains, abstains in relation to the Lord and gives thanks to God. (Rom. 14:5–6)

A great deal of scholarly effort has been invested in accounting for and closing the troublesome loopholes in this remarkably inclusive passage. Paul avoids all the technical terms associated with holy days, cultic calendars, or liturgical regulations. To "esteem one day over another" could refer to Sabbaths, Jewish festivals, required fast days, Lord's Day celebrations of the agape meal, or even lucky days calculated on the basis of astrology.[39] Raoul Dederen argues that Paul could not possibly have condoned breaking the Sabbath laws. He clearly states the reason for the problem in interpreting this verse, without indicating how it refutes his case. "Part of the interpretative problem of this passage is the fact that a linguistic study hardly contributes any substantial information toward a more accurate understanding."[40] I would contend that Paul's choice of insubstantial, vague language is intentional, and that exegetes disregard this choice and the direction of Paul's argument by imposing their own distinctions. Dederen inserts considerations that seem alien to this verse in order to make his case:

> The whole discussion concerns "unessentials," matters in which God has not spoken clearly in his Word. No such question can be conscientiously raised concerning the fundamental moral issues that are clarified in the Decalogue [including, of course, the Fourth Commandment about the Sabbath!], the Sermon on the Mount, or in any other plain statement of Scripture. Who can have a divine commandment before him and say to others: you can treat that commandment as you please; it really makes no difference whether you keep it or not; please yourselves? No apostle could so conduct an argument.[41]

The difficulty is that nowhere in this passage does Paul hint at the distinction between the essentials and the nonessentials of faith. Although Paul was fully capable of articulating subtle distinctions, he chose not to do so in this argument. The clear intention of his wording was to condone a range of options that might include everything from breaking the Fourth Commandment to astrology. By choosing so inclusive a formulation that no distinction could be made between essential and nonessential calendrical issues, Paul shifts the discussion to other considerations that are more directly related to the Christian gospel than the kind of legalistic reasoning that was driving hostile wedges between the house churches in Rome.

The first of these considerations is articulated in the admonition, "Let every one be fully convinced in his own mind" (Rom. 14:5). Each Christian has the responsibility to retain integrity in the quest for truth. The basis for this idea was stated in the great thesis concerning individual responsibility to determine right and wrong in Rom. 12:2, as Käsemann shows:

> What the apostle has in view is the renewed reason of 12:2 whose critical capacity leads through the call into a circum-

scribed sphere to firm conviction and resolute action on the basis of insight into one's own situation, and from that perspective remains open to new situations and the assessment of the brothers.[42]

The Christian process of decision-making, according to Paul, is not to be "conformed to this world" in the sense either of its social customs or of its religious laws, because each transformed Christian is to "prove" for himself or herself "what is the will of God, what is good and acceptable and perfect" (Rom. 12:2). The admonition to be "fully convinced" aims to protect the integrity of individual Christians, lest they feel impelled to conform to the standards of others rather than complying with their own. Paul had come to his own personal position in relation to holy days, and it was derived from his commitment as a missionary to be a Greek to the Greeks and a Jew to the Jews (I Cor. 9:21), an ethic so fraught with peril that Acts depicts him as simply being obedient to the Sabbath laws (Acts 17:2). But it is crucial to observe that he imposes neither of these ethical stances on his readers in Romans. The consideration that reveals the depth of his tolerant respect for the ethical integrity of others is the insistence that Christians should be truthful about their own standards and act accordingly.

A second consideration makes it plain that Paul is not simply advocating an ethic of absolute autonomy, in which each person acts to please himself. If some Roman Christians celebrate special days, they do so "in relation to the Lord." Once again, Paul's formulation is so inclusive that both sides could easily feel themselves included: he uses the term *phronein*, "be minded," which would have been a favorite term of self-description for the "strong" who thought of themselves as "the high-minded ones."[43] So whether one considers all days alike, as some of the strong did, or values one day more than another, as some of the weak did, for whatever reason, they all do it in honor of their Lord. Frédéric Godet captured the inclusive sense of

Paul's wording at this point: "The apostle means that the man who, in his religious practice, keeps the Jewish feast-days, does so for the purpose of doing homage to the Lord by resting in Him, as the man who does not observe them does so for the purpose of laboring actively for Him."[44] By placing the liturgical question within the context of the relationship to the Lord, Paul is able to protect the strong from the legalistic charge of breaking the Old Testament law or some other social custom while simultaneously legitimating the position of the weak by placing their obedience to the law in this relational context.

This second consideration, the relational basis of genuine tolerance, is driven home in the final lines of Rom. 14:6. Returning to the question of foods, Paul explains that the person who feels free to eat anything does so "in relation to the Lord, since he gives thanks to God." Likewise in the case of the weak, "he who does not eat does so in relation to the Lord, and he gives thanks to God." The one gives thanks for the meat and the wine, the other for the vegetables; what unites them in this carefully balanced rhetoric is not their liturgical or ethical preferences but their proper relationship to God. Rather than demonstrating the arrogant spirit of persons not yet aware of the gospel, as described in Rom 1:21ff., refusing to "honor him as God or give thanks to him," they find the basis of their mutual tolerance in their each giving praise to the only One to whom praise is due. By concentrating on their unity in relationship to God, Paul is able both to respect and to transcend the finally irresolvable question of doctrinal and liturgical differences.

We are now in a position to define what "welcome one another" means in terms of the classical theories of tolerance. Gustav Mensching distinguishes between two broad types of tolerance that have emerged in the history of religions. "Formal tolerance" is based on "unconcern" about either the doctrinal issues or the personal convictions that lead others to disagree with us.[45] One finds this kind of tolerance in the Renaissance adaptation of classical ideals,

in the Enlightenment tradition, and in the political arrange-
ments for tolerance that fall under the rubric of the "separation of church and state." As Glenn Tinder has made plain,
this is the type of tolerance found in John Locke, John
Stuart Mill, and modern liberalism. But clearly, this "live
and let live" form of tolerance is not what Paul is advocating in Romans. He is closer to the second broad type
described by Mensching, "actual positive tolerance" or
"intrinsic tolerance" such as that found in some of the
mystical religious traditions. It is willing to acknowledge
that the other person has convictions derived from genuine
encounters with the sacred. In this case the basis of tolerance is the transcendent sphere which no system of dogmas
can fully describe. A person rooted in this mystical tradition
can be tolerant so long as he or she discriminates sharply
between "truth as experienced reality" and "truth as rational correctness."[46] Since none can claim such final correctness, we find our unity in the reality that transcends us.

The difference between Paul's doctrine and Mensching's
could be summed up in the word "strenuous." To "welcome one another" means to reach out actively to include
others in one's circle, not simply to respect them and allow
them to stand on the outside. This aspect of Paul's thought
seems closer to Glenn Tinder's insistence that "the full
significance of tolerance becomes apparent only when it is
seen as openness between persons, readiness for relationships."[47] In his discussion of "Tolerance as Suffering,"
Tinder argues thus: "A human being is sustained by the
sympathetic interest of another. The interpretation of tolerance as communal implies that it must be a proffer of such
interest. . . . One of the main reasons for tolerance is to
permit the other to be present as he really is, veraciously
and responsibly. . . . A tolerant person 'puts up with' others,
but he does so attentively and thus upholds them."[48] This
involves, of course, forgiving others for offenses they commit by living according to different standards. From Tinder's philosophical standpoint, "the source of this capacity

[for forgiveness] is unclear."[49] But this is precisely where
Pauline thought makes its most decisive contribution. Paul
derives strenuous tolerance not from a soft theory of moral
relativism or a pragmatic adjustment to pluralistic reality or
in lofty ideals about the unity of all humankind in the
transcendent realm, but rather from the action of God in
Christ. Paul states this in the next clause of our pivotal text
(Rom. 15:7): "Welcome one another, therefore, *as Christ
has welcomed you . . .*"

IV

The grounding of Paul's concept of tolerance is so succinctly stated that its full significance could easily be
overlooked. Commentators tend to agree that the "as" in
15:7b indicates the reason why the Christians in Rome
should welcome one another: in effect, "since Christ has
welcomed you."[50] They occasionally observe that the idea
of Christ accepting both Jews and Gentiles, developed in
the following verses of ch. 15, derives from Rom. 9:1 to
11:36. John Knox paraphrases: "Just as Christ came under
the law in order that he might bring about the fulfillment of
God's purpose of salvation for both Jew and Gentile [which
has been set forth in chs. 9–11], you Gentiles should be
willing to bear with the scruples of some of your less
mature and less fully emancipated brethren."[51] The clause
"as Christ has welcomed you" also succinctly summarizes
the main argument of Romans, namely, that God accepts
sinners who formerly made themselves into his enemies,
and that they are justified by faith rather than by performance. The essence of the Christ event, as Paul depicts it in
Romans, was the "welcome" shown to God's enemies. All
humans have sinned, according to the opening chapters of
Romans, whether by violating the law and their own
conscience or by falling prey to pride. "For there is no
distinction," Paul writes in the climactic summary of ch. 3,
"since all have sinned and fall short of the glory of God;

they are justified by his grace as a gift, through the redemption which is in Christ Jesus" (Rom. 3:22–24). This statement is what a recent commentator terms the "fundamental idea of Romans. Everything that follows is explication."[52]

The theme of sinners and enemies to be "welcomed" by Christ also plays a central role in Romans 5. "But God shows his love for us in that while we were yet sinners Christ died for us." Indeed, "while we were enemies we were reconciled to God by the death of his Son" (Rom. 5:8, 10). Here the triumph of divine righteousness, and the justification of persons by faith alone, are described in simple, basic terms. It is a matter of God expressing his love to his enemies through the life and death of his Son. "Welcome one another, therefore, as Christ has welcomed you" directs us to pass on the same unconditional acceptance to others that we ourselves have already received. The tolerant ethic of Romans is thus integrally connected with faith.

The significance of this grounding of human tolerance in the love of God is clear when one compares it with current understandings of tolerance. John Murray Cuddihy accurately maintains that for most Protestant, Catholic, and Jewish thinkers in the recent American discussion, tolerance is no more than polite civility. It is expressed in the form of a grudging but polite admission that others should have the right to express themselves even if they are wrong. This attitude derives from American pluralism rather than from any coherent theory, according to Cuddihy. Since the conflicting claims to total truth by religious groups are mutually contradictory, the ultimate truth cannot be agreed upon. The best practical response is the meekly civil smile. The American civil religion, argues Cuddihy, is marked primarily by "rites of civility" which keep us from really encountering each other's beliefs and values. If we were really serious about such beliefs, we would not, in his opinion, be tolerant at all.[53]

The problem is basic, and thus far in the American

discussion the Pauline contribution has been overlooked. If tolerance rests simply on our failure to agree on the truth, then only the lukewarm and half-committed can share it. In that case, tolerance is possible only for those whose religious commitments are superficial. To put the dilemma more strongly, in the words of G. K. Chesterton: "Tolerance is the virtue of the man without convictions."[54]

But if Paul is correct, genuine tolerance of one's competitors is a logical step for those who are conscious that they themselves have been treated tolerantly by God. According to the argument of Romans, tolerance derives not from the weakness of faith but from its vital sense of its origin in the tolerant love of God.

Given the long argument in Romans that precedes the statement of tolerance in 15:7, it is clear that the words "as Christ has welcomed you" reflect a firm relationship and a fully internalized acceptance of a viewpoint. It is a basis of strength from which one can afford to "welcome others," to pass on the same generous relationship that one has been given. It thus provides what Harry Emerson Fosdick so perceptively grasped as the psychological clue to the intolerant campaigns of the 1920's: "Intolerance, personal or ecclesiastical, is an evidence of weakness. . . . The confident can afford to be calm and kindly; only the fearful must defame and exclude."[55] Those who have been set free from the fear that they are unwelcome, in other words, gain the inner freedom to welcome others. This is closely related to the discovery that psychologist Gordon Allport made in his study of prejudiced and unprejudiced adults several decades ago: "Tolerant children, it seems, are likely to come from homes with a permissive atmosphere. They feel welcome, accepted, loved, no matter what they do." In such homes, "the child does not have to guard every moment against impulses that might bring down parental wrath upon his head."[56]

Although Rom. 15:7 has not played a role in the advocacy of tolerance in Western culture, as we have seen, its logic underlies what Gustav Mensching has discovered to be a crucial mystical factor. Tolerance did not rise from the Protestant Reformers themselves, as he rightly insists, but from the pietistic and spiritualist fringes of the Reformation. In particular, the spiritualists "seek the union of God and man in a truly mystical fashion, by direct contact through the spirit. . . . Instead of objective, institutional authority they acknowledge the 'inner light' as the only way to enlightenment and revelation, and this is their basis for intrinsic tolerance over against others."[57] Mensching cites the Quakers as typical representatives of this Christian mysticism which "reflects the sort of religious immediacy reported of the spirit-inspired congregations of early Christianity. Such religious ideas allow us to understand why the Quakers have always passionately advocated intrinsic tolerance and still do so."[58] Pauline mysticism as expressed in the clause "as Christ has welcomed you" is a product of such early Christian congregational life, in which unity was derived from a common experience of grace rather than from a uniform creed or social style.

I would also suggest that the logic of Rom. 15:7 is implicit in the practical tolerance manifest in the Wesleyan tradition. The famous statement of John Wesley to his rival and theological adversary George Whitefield is more than mere accommodationism. "If your heart is as my heart, give me your hand" meant that there is unity in the experience of faith, in which persons are led to accept the reality of God's love for them despite their failures. It is not that Wesley's heart felt particular warmth toward his rival, but that it had been "strangely warmed" by the Spirit to discover a "welcome" in the heart of God that he knew no one could possibly deserve. The logic of this vitally experiential doctrine of tolerance was caught by some of the Wesley hymns, written and sung at a time when the connection between human love and divine love was more intensely grasped than it has been in much of the later Wesleyan tradition. Charles Wesley's hymn with the title "Christ,

from Whom All Blessings Flow" contains lines that appropriately conclude our discussion of "as Christ has welcomed you":

> Sweetly may we all agree,
>   Touched with loving sympathy,
> Kindly for each other care;
>   Every member feel its share.
>
> Love, like death, hath all destroyed,
>   Rendered all distinctions void;
> Names and sects and parties fall:
>   Thou, O Christ, art all-in-all! [59]

V

This leads me to the final point, the purpose clause of our
text. "Welcome one another, therefore, as Christ has welcomed you, *for the glory of God.*" Tolerance within the
Christian community, according to Paul, gives glory to God.
When one places this idea in the context of the tightly knit
argument of Romans, a tolerant welcome among the competing house churches in Rome would reveal that God had
regained control of self-centered groups, that his love was
now animating them. For just as the welcome of Christ does
not wait for the transformation of the sinner, but expresses
itself unconditionally to those who have made themselves
enemies, so the competing groups in Rome could accept
each other without demanding conformity. Ernst Kühl
suggests that this had a decisive racial connotation for the
original audience at Rome. The theme of Jewish-Gentile
relations that is developed in 15:8–13 defines the context of
15:7 so that, according to Kühl, the mutual welcome per-
tains to the conflict between Jewish Christians and Gentile
Christians. It is in this situation that the motif of glorifying
God is to be understood: "The work of Christ for Jews and
Gentiles alike served the glory of God, in order that both,
Jews and Gentiles, would be able to praise God in the same

congregation, with one accord and one voice."[60]

It is important to observe that the connection between mutual welcome and glory does not imply uniformity in the sense that all factions in the church must now agree to a single doctrinal or liturgical standard. The nineteenth-century commentator Godet explains: "Unity in the works of God is never uniformity. Rather harmony implies variety. This common adoration, in which all presently existing contrasts in the church are to be fused, does not prevent each group in the new people of God from bringing with it its own experiences, and playing its particular part in the final concert."[61]

In other words, the conservatives in Rome did not have to become liberal, and the Jews did not have to become Greek. Their love would transcend these basic differences and allow the natural uniqueness of race and temperament to flourish. What God had created and redeemed would thus come into its own, and he would be glorified if they welcomed each other as Christ had welcomed them.

The startling significance of all this is lost if we forget that Paul's use of "glory" reverses most of the Biblical tradition in one regard. Most Jewish and Christian writers and thinkers assumed that God's glory would be manifest only in the total victory of the good over evil. One sees this in Psalm 79, where God is asked, "Pour out thy anger on the nations that do not know thee," because they have "devoured Jacob [i.e., Israel], and laid waste his habitation." The military reversal is requested in the line, "Help us, O God of our salvation, for the glory of thy name; deliver us, and forgive our sins, for thy name's sake!" The same connection is visible in Psalm 149, where the Lord is celebrated as the one who adorns his humble people with victory so that they can "exult in glory." They are to take "two-edged swords in their hands, to wreak vengeance on the nations and chastisement on the peoples, . . . to execute on them the judgment written! This is glory for all his faithful ones."

This is a crucial element in American as well as ancient Israelite culture. The most stirring battle song of the North during the Civil War celebrates precisely this traditional theme: "Mine eyes have seen the glory of the coming of the Lord; He is trampling out the vintage where the grapes of wrath are stored." The idea is that in the victorious armies of the "good side," God's glory makes itself visible.[62] The same motif, secularized, plays a key role in the popular entertainments of our culture. In episode after episode, the triumph of superheroes of comic books, television, and film provides the climax of dramatic action.[63] The nature of the modern superhero is such that total victory is both required and expected; it reveals his or her power and "super" aura, just as victory over evil was thought to reveal the aura of God for ancient Israel.

This is precisely what Paul reverses in Rom. 15:7. It is not in the victory of the weak over the strong, or vice versa, says Paul, but in their mutual, tolerant welcome that the glory of God is manifest. This theme of God's glory sets the entire question of tolerance in a healthy context, guarding against the misunderstandings that have so frequently arisen throughout Judeo-Christian history. To give glory to God is to place humans in their rightful place as creatures whom it is always dangerous to glorify. To grasp this distinction is to acknowledge the transcendence of God, whose glory always surpasses our small programs and agendas. In this sense, the "glory" of God stands for the transcendent though "elusive presence"—to use Samuel Terrien's expression[64]—who acts always to keep human arrogance in bounds. It is when vital faith in such a transcendent Lord issues in strenuous tolerance of fellow humans that the Lord is genuinely glorified.

Chapter II

CONSCIENCE AND THE MEASURING ROD OF FAITH

One of the primary sources of the tolerance doctrine in Western culture is the idea of liberty of conscience. In contrast to the medieval assumption that conscience should be viewed as legitimate only if it was grounded in dogmatic truth as officially defined, the idea of an autonomous conscience began to emerge in the so-called "left wing" of the Protestant Reformation. It was worked out in classical form by Sebastian Castellio, the polemicist whose writings were provoked by the burning of Servetus in Geneva. According to Roland Bainton, Castellio "defined conscience as loyalty to that which one believes to be right, even though objectively one may be in error." In Castellio's view, says Bainton, "Servetus was put to death for telling the truth. Had he been willing to recant and speak against his conscience, he might have escaped. He was executed because he would not lie." Bainton goes on to observe that "scarcely anything in the teaching of Castellio was more radical than this. He relativized conscience." Although Castellio's dictum, "To force conscience is worse than cruelly to kill a man," was understood and accepted only after the passage of more than a century,[1] it eventually became one of the foundations of the liberal doctrine of tolerance.

Neither Castellio nor his later devotees were aware of the remarkable congruity of this idea of the autonomous conscience with the thought of Paul. Its New Testament foundation was instead the Golden Rule of Jesus.[2] Werner Kaegi's study on Castellio and the beginnings of tolerance in the sixteenth century concludes that the basis of his doctrine was exclusively the example of Christ in following the love commandment.[3]

One gains a similar impression from reading the literature concerning Roger Williams. To cite Bainton again: "Williams stoutly defended the integrity of the mistaken. His supporting evidences were relatively few. . . . Williams' argument was simply that those who by common consent of the Puritans were actually in error were nonetheless as devoted and as sacrificial as those deemed to be correct. And if devoted and if sacrificial, then to be regarded as sincere."[4] Williams wrote Governor Endicott that "[what] we call conscience is of such a nature . . . that although it be groundless, false, and deluded, yet it is not by any arguments or torments easily removed. . . . I speak of conscience, a persuasion fixed in the mind and heart of a man, which enforceth him to judge (as Paul said of himself a persecutor) and to do so and so, with respect to God."[5] He went on to describe the courage of Catholic and Protestant martyrs as a sign of genuine faith. The example of Paul's persecution of the early Christians arose later in the letter where the words of Christ on the Damascus road were rephrased to drive home the issue of conscience: "Endicot, Endicot, why huntest thou me? . . . Is it possible (may you well say) that since I hunt, I hunt not the life of my Saviour, and the blood of the Lamb of God. I have fought against many several sorts of consciences, is it beyond all possibility and hazard, that I have not fought against God, that I have not persecuted Jesus in some of them."[6] There is a potential relationship between this argument and Paul's concept of conscience in I Corinthians, but Williams never developed it.

We encounter here an oddity in the development of the idea of conscience in the Western world that is similar in some regards to the avoidance of Romans by advocates of pluralism. In this instance the explanation is probably to be found in the complexity of Paul's discussion of conscience in I Corinthians 8 and 10. It has required more than a hundred years of intensive scholarly discussion, using all the techniques of historical-critical methods and historical-religious comparisons, to discover the contours of Paul's approach to conscience and their relation to questions raised by the Corinthian factions.[7] It was virtually impossible for earlier thinkers, anchored in classical and medieval thought patterns, to overcome their prior assumptions about the nature of conscience to the extent of grasping Paul's original and remarkably modern view.[8] Not only did he defend conscience even when it errs, but he viewed it as socially conditioned and intimately connected with the mechanisms of self-respect, moral autonomy, and psychic health. By dissociating conscience from the direct voice of God or the rational principle, he was able to face the evidence of what depth psychologists might call a "conscience lag," in which the prior conditioning of tradition and upbringing prevented some early Christians from acting in the light of the freedom they had been given through the gospel. His resultant doctrine of protecting the conscience of the "weak" thus provides a decisive bulwark in defense of tolerance in its most modern sense.

We will begin by sketching the contours of Paul's remarkable approach to conscience and then move to connect it with the concepts of "sober-mindedness" and "the measuring rod of faith" in Romans.

I

When one places the Pauline letters in chronological order, the word *suneidēsis* ("conscience") does not appear at all until a section of the Corinthian correspondence.[9] In fact, nine of the fifteen occurrences of the word in the Pauline corpus appear in this section. Since Paul uses words like "heart" in the earlier letters to depict the conscience, it seems probable that *suneidēsis* entered into the discussion because of special circumstances within the Corinthian church. As we piece the evidence together, the situation there was as follows. A debate seems to have arisen concerning the advisability of eating meat offered to idols. A conservative group in the church strongly opposed this because, being former pagans themselves, they felt that eating such meat constituted entering into communion with the idols. They therefore experienced conscience pangs whenever they ate this meat and since most meat sold in the pagan marketplaces was similarly tainted, this became a rather troubling issue. This group seems to have sent the question which Paul answers in I Cor. 10:23ff., i.e., Should not one examine meat on account of conscience to determine whether it has been offered to idols? In opposition to this conservative group in Corinth there was a group of radical spiritual enthusiasts who scoffed at scruples. This group can be termed "Gnostic" because its members conceived of salvation in terms of knowledge of their spiritual essence and because of their consistently dualistic world view.[10] They scorned the unenlightened conscience of conservatives and embarked on a vigorous campaign to educate them. Their method was to destroy the supposed misconceptions of the "weak conscience" by goading the conservatives into open violation of their scruples about the idol meat. This group also sent a question that Paul discusses in I Cor. 8:1–13, i.e., Should not the conscience of the weak be edified?

With this background in mind, we can turn to the passages themselves. The word *suneidēsis* appears first in I Corinthians 8, where the question posed by the Gnostics is being discussed. Paul evidently had been reminded in the Corinthians' letter to him that according to his own teaching the idols were nothing and as a consequence all food offered to them could be eaten without hesitation. So he opens the discussion by admitting the basic correctness of the Gnostic position (8:1ff.). His argument may be paraphrased as follows: "We all have knowledge that the idols are nothing and that all food comes from God alone. But not everyone has assimilated this knowledge, for some persons' consciences continue to be aroused when they eat sacrificial meat. When such persons are induced by the Gnostics' provocative example to eat despite their conscience, they are not edified but instead destroyed. Thus one's knowledge must be guided by love so that the weak brother is not led to stumble."

The word *suneidēsis* appears three times in this discussion, embedded each time in a different expression. Each of these expressions is usually translated with the words "weak conscience," but this overlooks the masculine participle and adjective in I Cor. 8:10, which requires the translation "his conscience, he himself being weak..." The question of why Paul distinguishes between the conscience and the weak man in v. 10, whereas he refers without hesitation to the "weak conscience" in vs. 7 and 12, must be dealt with in connection with the often-expressed view that Paul ironically paraphrases a sentence from the Corinthians' letter in v. 10.[11] If one were to reconstruct the Gnostic expression to which Paul alludes in this verse, the result would be: "Should his weak conscience not be edified?" Such a question would evoke an automatic affirmative answer, so Paul rephrases it in order to distinguish between the conscience, which is edified, and the man himself, who remains weak. He also subtly reduces the positive connotation of "edify" by appending the clause, "to eat meat offered to idols," which implies that the conscience was not really edified but was merely led to acquiesce in an act which at best was theologically inconsequential (v. 8) and which under these conditions was destructive (v. 11). The distinction between the weak person and a supposedly edified conscience serves to express the inner disunity that results when someone acts against conscience. The dissolution of personal unity expressed here was hinted at by the juxtaposition of I Cor. 8:1 ("we know that all have the knowledge") with v. 7a ("but not all have the knowledge"). Even the "weak" in Corinth had the theoretical knowledge that the idols were powerless, but they were unable to act on this knowledge because of the continuing influence of their inherited dread. This lag in assimilation could be aggravated, according to v. 10, into a disjunction between self and conscience, so that the result was a person's destruction (v. 11).

If this analysis of Paul's ironic alteration of the Gnostic expression in I Cor. 8:10 is correct, the Pauline and the Gnostic understandings of conscience may be rather sharply distinguished. The Gnostics were so concerned to build up the weak conscience that they did not hesitate to incite the less-enlightened members of the congregation into acting against their scruples. Paul, in contrast, rejects the idea of directly edifying the conscience and encourages those with a "weak conscience" to act according to their own standards and so to avoid pain. For the Gnostic, an enlightened conscience was apparently a prerequisite for salvation, whereas for Paul it was not. The difference in approach is most apparent in their respective understandings of the word "weak." For the Gnostics, persons with a weak conscience could not enjoy salvation because of their continued bondage to the material sphere. The Gnostic associated "power" with the realm of the "spirit" and "weakness" with the realm of the "flesh." By associating "knowledge" and "spirit" the Gnostic assumed that persons with a "weak conscience" lacked the saving knowledge of their spiritual origin. Thus a "weak conscience" carried the connotation of being unenlightened.

Paul accepts this Gnostic understanding of the weak conscience as unenlightened but he draws some very different conclusions. Having used the word "weak" in a rather loose fashion in the earlier epistles to depict sickness (Phil. 2:26, Gal. 4:13) or powerlessness (Gal. 4:9, I Thess. 5:14), Paul develops it into a theological category in Corinthians and in the later epistles. The "word of the cross" is referred to as "the weakness of God," which was more powerful than the wisdom and might of the world (I Cor. 1:25); God elected "the weak things of the world" in order to shame the wise and powerful (I Cor. 1:27); it follows of course that possession of a weak conscience would not disqualify one for salvation. Here we encounter Paul's theological motivation for respecting the autonomy of the weak conscience. It must be respected, not because it places upon humans a claim whose authority rests in the transcendent realm,[12] but because of God's revelation of himself in weakness and his election of weak persons. Since God has elected those with a weak conscience, Paul calls for love and renunciation on the part of the "strong" as the appropriate response to divine action.

Out of Paul's respect for the "weak" comes a much more adequate understanding of their situation than the Gnostics had. Whereas the Gnostics naively assumed that the injection of right knowledge would solve the problem, on the apparent assumption that the conscience and the spiritual self were identical, Paul takes into consideration the possibility of a lag caused by cultural and psychological conditioning (I Cor. 8:7; *sunētheia*=conditioning by custom). He confronts the inexplicable fact that the "weak" have the knowledge and yet do not have it; he takes account of the destruction of the self that comes when one disobeys one's own conscience. The terms Paul uses to describe such destruction are quite revealing. In I Cor. 8:7 he states that the conscience becomes "contaminated," which means that it bears the painful knowledge of sin. In 8:12 Paul refers to a "wounding" of the conscience, which appears to denote a disabling of the function of the conscience. Since this verse is an elaboration of 8:11 ("this weak man is destroyed . . ."), Paul considers the result of such disabling wounds to be the destruction of the person. This leads us back to 8:10, where Paul distinguishes between the conscience, which was supposedly edified, and the person, who remained weak.

Clearly, in every instance, Paul assumes that the conscience possesses an autonomy which separates it in some sense from the ego of the person. Its function is to guard the integrity of the person, and when its autonomy is disregarded, the person is dangerously divided within.

The next passage where the word "conscience" appears is in a later section of Corinthians. After describing the apostolic example of the exercise and renunciation of freedom in relation to both the "weak" and the "strong" in I Cor. 9:1–23, Paul returns in 10:23 to 11:1 to the problem of sacrificial meat. Here the word *suneidēsis* appears five times. Paul commands both the "weak" and the "strong" to eat meat from the market or in a pagan home without examination of its source on account of conscience, since all food comes from the Creator. But if one should learn that the meat was from a pagan sacrifice, then one should refrain from eating in order to spare the conscience of the "weak."

Within this argument the word *suneidēsis* appears repeatedly in such formal expressions that a citation of the Corinthians' letter to Paul has often been suspected. Not only is the clause "without raising questions on account of conscience" repeated twice (I Cor. 10:25, 27) but the phrase "on account of the conscience" is appended to the end of an already completed expression in 10:28. Assuming that the informer in this verse is one of the "weak" Christians, one must ask with Johannes Weiss[13] why Paul didn't write "on account of *his* conscience" and why he appended "conscience" with "and" as if the informer and the informer's conscience were somehow distinct. The separation of "that man who informed you" from "the conscience" is strikingly similar to the distinction we noted in 8:10 between the conscience and the man himself, who remains weak. The reason for the distinction between the informer and the conscience in 10:28 becomes clear when one observes who is being addressed at this point. Since only the "weak" Christian would have been interested in informing a friend at dinner, and since the person being addressed is apparently in no danger of hurting his or her own conscience, it must be the "strong" who are addressed here. Since Paul is again addressing the Gnostics, the distinction between the conscience and the self serves to contradict the Gnostic assumptions and to insist that the conscience is an autonomous agent and cannot be treated as identical with the self.

It is interesting to note, however, that although Paul speaks to the Gnostics at this point, he uses the word "conscience" with a different connotation than in the earlier discussion of their question in I Corinthians 8. Here in ch. 10 the word is used in the phrase "on account of the conscience," which implies that the very presence of "conscience" in connection with the meat was painful. This is understandable on the basis of Pierce's discovery of the "moral-bad-absolute" connotation of conscience in Hellenistic culture.[14] Here *suneidēsis* connotes not the agency of awareness of one's misdeeds, but rather the painful awareness itself. This reflects the fact that the question posed by the "weak" about whether they should examine meat on account of conscience made use of the word *suneidēsis* to depict the painful knowledge of transgression. This indicates that the conservatives in Corinth did not have the same conception of conscience as the Gnostics did. The Gnostics thought of *suneidēsis* as the agent of awareness about misconduct and were interested in identifying the conscience with the spiritual self, whereas the "weak" party in Corinth thought of it as the painful knowledge of misconduct.

Paul's interest in autonomy is reflected in the plan he sets forth in this section (I Cor. 10:23 to 11:1) for the gradual education of the conscience in reference to eating sacrificial meat. In issuing the command to eat whatever is bought in the market without examination of its origin, he places a radical obligation upon the "weak" Christians to overcome their scruples. We know that almost all meat that could be procured in a Hellenistic marketplace had some connection with a pagan cult. In not anxiously examining the origin of the meat they purchase, the "weak" are to act on the principle that "The earth is the Lord's and the fullness thereof" (I Cor. 10:26). But the unspoken assumption is that they will, in waiving prior investigation, take for granted that the particular piece of meat before them was not sacrificial. For in issuing precisely the same advice regarding eating in a pagan home, Paul rules that if one is informed that the meat is sacrificial, then one ought to avoid eating it so as not to lead the "weak" to act against their conscience. As questionable as it might appear to the moralist, one cannot avoid the fact that Paul is operating on the principle that what you don't know won't hurt you. His plan is for those with a weak (i.e., unfree) conscience to practice the principle "All things are lawful" by not inquiring concerning the origin of what they eat; but the moment they discover it is sacrificial, they are to desist so as not to defile or bruise their conscience. The autonomy and inviolability of the conscience lie at the root of his ethic at this point. Having opposed in I Corinthians 8 the attempt to undermine the judgment of the weak conscience by violent enlightenment, Paul sets forth in I Cor. 10:23ff. a plan to exercise freedom while leaving the veto power of the conscience untouched.

It is in the light of this insistence upon the autonomy of the individual conscience that the literary and logical problems of I Cor. 10:29b–30 must be discussed. The passage is as follows:

> For why should my freedom be judged by another person's conscience? If I partake [of sacrificial meat] with thankfulness, why am I defamed for eating food over which I have said grace?

Three basic interpretations have been suggested for this section: (1) It is an objection expressed by "strong" Christians to a renunciation of their freedom, inserted either by a later editor or by Paul himself as a sort of rhetorical question.[15] (2) It is a warning to the "weak" not to take advantage of the "strong" Christians' renunciation of their freedom by attempting to enslave them or denounce their freedom.[16] (3) It is Paul's explanation of his advice not to eat in I Cor. 10:28–29a; one should set aside one's freedom for the moment so as not to allow it to come under judgment or denunciation at the hands of the "weak."[17]

The first interpretation is unacceptable because any objection to Paul's advice in I Cor. 10:28–29a would be introduced by "but" instead of "for"; the wording of vs. 29b–30 is too thoroughly Pauline to be an interpolation;[18] and if Paul inserted an objection of the "strong" in the form of a question, then why is no answer provided in the succeeding verses? The second alternative is likewise incapable of clarifying the presence of "for" in v. 29b, and it is revealing that those who propose this interpretation avoid providing a precise translation. As much as one's personal sympathies may rest with this second alternative, it must be set aside. It is thus on the basis of the third alternative that the exegesis of the phrase "by another person's conscience" must be worked out. Since this verse provides the rationale for Paul's advice to spare the conscience of the "weak" in the preceding verse, it is apparent that "another person's" refers to someone with a weak conscience. In the light of the use of the word elsewhere in Corinthians, the verb appears to mean "to judge" rather than "to examine" or "to investigate." The word "conscience" is therefore used in this verse in a slightly different fashion than we have encountered heretofore. Instead of referring to the knowledge or pain that a person has after a misdeed, it appears at first glance to be the agent of judgment upon someone else's acts: "For why should my freedom be judged by another person's conscience?"[19] Paul considers such judgment by an alien conscience to be so abhorrent that it must be avoided, for only under this assumption could 10:29b provide the motivation for the advice in v. 28, as the word "for" indicates.

The puzzle with this third interpretation is that the "weak" persons who heretofore have had to be protected by the "strong" so that they would not act against their conscience suddenly appear in I Cor. 10:29b–30 as rigid bigots who pass judgment upon the "strong," condemning their freedom and piety. Although Paul deals with a group of "weak" Christians in Romans 14–15 who are quite articulate in their condemnation of the "strong," this is the first time such an aggressive attitude on the part of the "weak" is even implied in Corinthians.[20] In fact, nowhere in I Corinthians is there evidence that allows us to think of the "weak" as vituperous bigots. Thus the "judgment" and "defamation" that Paul seeks to avoid cannot have come from persons who do not eat sacrificial meat and who condemn those who do. Instead, it is a "judgment" that comes when the weak are induced to eat by the example of the "strong," so that the resultant pains of conscience are blamed on the "strong." The "weak" feel they have sinned, and they naturally project this feeling onto those who induced them to eat. They quite naturally hold the freedom of the "strong" responsible for the pain that has been incurred. If such "weak" persons are destroyed, their fate will rightly be placed on the account of the "strong." In this way the "strong" are open to defamation from all sides because their eating of the food as God's gift has become the means of others' destruction. The Greek word "blaspheme" ("why am I blasphemed?" I Cor. 10:30) is thus understandable in this context as a defamation of that which is good. The word "conscience" in 10:29b is therefore not that which marks the misdeeds of others but rather is the weak person's knowledge of his or her own sin, which in this case may be projected to implicate the strong in guilt. Yet the most impressive aspect of this section is Paul's abhorrence of coming under the judgment of another person's conscience. His concern to maintain the autonomy of the individual conscience expresses itself not only in the command to spare the "weak" but also in the advice for the "strong" to avoid letting themselves be judged or defamed by others.

Now we are in a position to tie together the strands of Paul's approach to the problem of conscience. We have noted that both parties in Corinth posed questions to Paul regarding the conscience, and that a differing conception of conscience was presupposed by each question. In I Corinthians 8 Paul dealt with the Gnostic question about edifying the conscience of the weak, and here the word *suneidēsis* connotes the self as the agent of knowledge. In ch. 10, however, Paul dealt with the question formulated by the "weak" so that *suneidēsis* in these verses connotes the painful awareness of transgression. Both definitions were current in the Hellenistic world at that time, and no distinction was usually made between them. Yet Paul implicitly rejects the Gnostic identification of the conscience with the spiritual self and insists upon the autonomous function of the conscience. The conscience is not subject to education or manipulation in any direct fashion, even by the person whose conscience it is. Any education of the conscience must proceed slowly and indirectly while respecting the veto power of the conscience at all times. One reason Paul gives for thus respecting the autonomy of the conscience is that even those with a weak, i.e., unenlightened, conscience have been elected by God and thus have intrinsic dignity in his sight. But one suspects that a more fundamental reason is hinted at in both ch. 8 and ch. 10, where the death-dealing schizophrenia is described. Behind this seems to lie the Hebraic assumption of the primary importance of personal unity.[21] The conscience appears here as the defender of personal integrity. To act without regard to one's own conscience is to enter into destruction through the dissolution of the self. At any event, Paul never explains the autonomy of the conscience in terms of its relation to God, but as a purely human function, equally at work and equal in validity in believer or unbeliever, "strong" or "weak."

II

Since the several references to conscience in Romans have played so great a role in forming the traditional "voice of God" view, it is essential that their interpretation should also be clarified. In Romans 2:15 and 9:1 the term "conscience" is used with the verb "to witness with,"[22] which has led traditional interpreters to the view that conscience is the divine witness of right and wrong that works inside every human. The logical implications of this interpretation are devastating: If conscience is the divine witness, it cannot err. If its witness differs from the revelation of God's will through the established church, it cannot be a legitimate conscience and therefore requires the correction of the authorities. As the Puritan divines said in arguing this point, "We shall keep your conscience." That such a view— with its disastrous impact on the concept of tolerance— retains its appeal is evident in the authoritative article by Christian Maurer.[23] His understanding of the Pauline concept of conscience does not take the situational use of Paul's anthropological terms into account. Rather than interpreting the earlier Corinthian usage in the light of Romans, it is important to place each letter in its historical setting and to take account of the unique contours of meaning within that context.

In the case of Rom. 2:15, the misunderstanding of conscience is intertwined with a translation problem that is more suitably discussed in a more technical monograph.[24] I follow Godet, Sanday and Headlam, and others in separating the clauses in this verse in a literal fashion. Paul is explaining that Gentiles have a moral sense even though they do not have the Jewish law, and he cites in this verse several indications that this is so: (1) "What the law requires is written on their hearts," presumably through social conditioning. (2) "Their conscience also bears witness" when they violate their moral standards. (3) "Their conflicting thoughts accuse or perhaps excuse them" in that their powers of intellectual discrimination are constantly active. A proper grasp of the grammatical structure of this sentence confirms that "conscience" is used in a manner that is basically consistent with its use in I Corinthians. Scholars have observed that conscience is assumed to have a definite autonomy in this sentence, in that the person does not act as its subject.[25] Adolf Schlatter describes with precision the separation between the person thinking the conflicting thoughts and the conscience: "Next to the speaking 'I' the conscience stands forth as an independent entity, which does not allow itself to be influenced by the speaker."[26]

It seems to me that in fact Paul is describing three rather different aspects of the moral life in this verse. These are (1) the largely unconscious standard that has been internalized through education and cultural conditioning; (2) the conscience itself, which involuntarily registers whether this standard is being followed in a particular action; and (3) the conscious reasoning process, which evaluates alternative courses of action. Paul's argument is that the objective presence of these moral factors in the lives of Gentiles proves that they are accountable. It is therefore appropriate for them to stand before the bar of justice at the end of time: "on that day when, according to my gospel, God judges the secrets of men by Christ Jesus" (Rom. 2:16). There is no hint in this passage that Paul thought of conscience as the direct voice of God. Rather, the conscience is viewed as the autonomous capacity within humans that marks their consistency with whatever moral standard they have internalized.

There are close verbal similarities between Rom. 2:15 ("their conscience also bears witness") and Rom. 9:1 ("I am not lying, my conscience bears me witness in the Holy Spirit"). The verb "to witness with" is used in both instances to indicate independent confirmation of a principle or a state of mind. In 9:1 it confirms that Paul is not

dishonest when he says, despite allegations to the contrary,
"I have great sorrow and unceasing anguish in my heart . . .
for the sake of my brethren, my kinsmen by race" (9:2–3).
When one carefully analyzes the grammatical structure of
this verse, it is clear that the witness of conscience is
connected to the statement "I am not lying."[27] Conscience
in this instance does not witness independently to the pain
of Paul.[28] The conscience, as always, is basically a negative
voice—the knowledge one has "with oneself" that a deed
just performed is inconsistent with one's standard. Here
Paul's standard is telling the truth, and he simply affirms
that the silence of his conscience indicates he is not lying.
If conscience were not an autonomous capacity within
humans, the argument would not hold. Paul is able to
distinguish in himself between the conscience and the "I"
who claims to be telling the truth and then confesses to the
depth of his anguish about his fellow Jews. Although it is
the person himself who knows the consistency of his own
deeds with his internalized standard of conduct, such
knowledge is involuntary to the extent that the conscience
can be cited as an independent witness over against the
self.[29]

The unique and misleading feature of Rom. 9:1 as far as
the history of research and of the conscience concept in
Western culture is concerned is the reference to the Holy
Spirit. Some have argued that this implies that the conscience witnesses in behalf of the spirit[30] or is controlled by
the spirit.[31] In fact, as the parallelism in Paul's statement
reveals, the "in Christ" of 9:1a corresponds to "in the Holy
Spirit" in 9:1c with the purpose of lending solemnity to an
oath formula.[32] In explaining the "oathlike assurances" of
Paul's integrity, Nils Dahl points out the intense personal
involvement and the close relation of this theme to "the
epistolary situation" in that "one of the purposes is to refute
false rumors that Paul had rejected the Law and his own
people."[33] The insertion of the phrase "in the Holy Spirit"
reveals that in this particular instance, despite the normally

erring quality of conscience, it is in full harmony with the Holy Spirit.[34] To make this reference in Romans the interpretative axis of Paul's entire view of conscience, as has traditionally been done, is to disregard the unique argumentative requirements that Paul faced in Romans and to level off the differing contours of the rest of Paul's usage.

III

Once a person is sensitized to the striking emphasis on the autonomy of limited, human conscience in Pauline thought, the route to clearing up the misunderstanding about "the measuring rod of faith" in Rom. 12:3 is open. The usual translation is ambiguous about whether "measure" means a quantity or a principle of measurement; it also disguises the crucial play on the term "minded." Here is the RSV translation: "I bid every one among you not to think of himself more highly than he ought to think, but to think with sober judgment, each according to the measure of faith which God has assigned him." One would never be able to infer from this translation that "minded" appears four times in different combinations, revealing the horizon of a sophisticated philosophical and religious debate concerning the limits and exercise of human autonomy. My literal translation, though lacking in felicity, helps to focus the issue:

> For by the grace given to me I bid every one among you not to be super-minded above what one ought to be minded, but to set your mind on being sober-minded, each according to the measuring rod of faith that God has dealt out. (Rom. 12:3)

A major weakness in the interpretation of this passage by the standard commentaries is that the classical Greek background connecting "measure" with "sobriety" is not taken into account.[35] Helen North's study of "sober-mindedness" has shown that from the time of the ancient Greek city-states, pride was viewed as the vice of tyrants and *sophrō-sunē*, "moderation" or "sobriety," the virtue of mature

civility.[36] The distinction was that the one refuses to acknowledge limits, while the other incorporates the ancient
Delphic ideal, "Know thyself that thou art but mortal."
Johanna Schmidt has studied the connection between these
ideas and the tradition of "measure and harmony" in Greek
thought, showing the dangers that were discovered in the
idea that "man is the measure of all things."[37] Hans Dieter
Betz has shown the relevance of this background for Paul's
parallel discussion in II Corinthians 10–13, making it clear
that he both understood and utilized the Socratic tradition
with its Delphic roots.[38] It is therefore no longer plausible
to set this background aside on the traditional grounds that
Paul was hostile to philosophy. In a decisive way, Paul's
view of faith in Rom. 12:3 was shaped by a creative
interaction with this philosophical legacy as it related to the
problem of differing conscience structures and theological
aggression between members of the early congregations.

When the classical background is overlooked, commentators gain the impression that "faith" is used differently in
Rom. 12:3 from the way it is used in the earlier argument of
Romans. F. F. Bruce writes: " 'Faith' here has a rather
different sense from that which it has in the earlier part of
the Epistle; here it denotes the spiritual power given to
each Christian."[39] C. E. B. Cranfield tries to pare back the
seeming difference between Rom. 12:3 and the doctrinal
use of the word "faith" in Romans 1–8, insisting that it
implies for the Christian "a standard (by which to measure,
estimate, himself), namely, his faith in the sense of . . . the
basic Christian response to God."[40] In other words, on the
premise that "faith" in Romans denoted the objective
doctrines that must be believed, Paul here is imposing a
single standard on all. Since Cranfield is conscious of the
danger of raising a contradiction between this verse and the
tolerant diversity of Romans 14–15, he bends the doctrinal
standard in a flexible direction that ultimately threatens the
singularity of the single "standard" he thinks Paul had in
mind. The rather tortured result is as follows: "Every

member of the church, instead of thinking of himself more
highly than he ought, is so to think of himself as to think
soberly, measuring himself by the standard which God has
given him in his faith, that is, by a standard which forces
him to concentrate his attention on those things in which he
is on precisely the same level as his fellow Christians, . . .
for the standard Paul has in mind consists, we take it, not in
the relative strength or otherwise of the particular Christian's faith but in the simple fact of its existence, that is, on
the fact of his admission of his dependence on, and commitment to, Jesus Christ."[41] In such explanations, which could
be multiplied many times in the Romans commentaries of
various theological and linguistic traditions, the echoes of
centuries of battle concerning heresy and orthodoxy are
perceptible. There must be one faith, and when Paul uses
the term here in a way that seems to threaten this unity,
theological arsenals are rolled out to prove that the threat
cannot be real.

When one takes account of the classical Greek background and reflects on its relevance for the struggles in the
early Christian churches, the plain meaning of Paul's language comes to light. As Betz showed in the parallel
passage in II Cor. 10:13–16, Paul in fact relies on the
Delphic/Socratic tradition of keeping to one's measure and
not falling prey to pride. Paul was conscious that some in
the church had a measure or standard different from his (II
Cor. 10:16) that ought legitimately to be followed. On the
question of missionary strategy, for example, Paul insists
only that each group keep to the limits agreed upon. Both in
II Cor. 10:13 and in Rom. 12:3 the term "measure" (metron)
is connected with "distribute, deal out" in the past tense,
which implies an event in which God conveyed to each a
sense of mission and limits. This term strongly suggests the
principle of individuation, implying that each Christian is
given a peculiar principle of measurement.[42] This impression is strengthened by the prominent location of the
inclusive "each one" in Rom. 12:3. There is no hint that

some have a superior or more fully authenticated "faith" than others. The word "measure" *(metron)* is as ambiguous in Greek as in English, meaning either an "instrument of measuring" or "the result of measuring, quantity, number."[43] The choice must be made on the basis of the context, and in this case the connection with "deal out" and "each" makes it clear which route to follow. It is the classic philosophical sense of keeping to the measuring rod or limit, not falling prey to pride.

The idea in Rom. 12:3 is thus consistent with the principle of varying conscience structures. It provides the essential premise for the argument we sketched in Chapter I on the basis of Romans 14–15, that the "weak" should follow one standard and the "strong" another. "The measuring rod of faith" is the norm that each person is provided in the appropriation of the grace of God. Although faith in its proper sense is the relationship of holding fast to the grace of God, it includes a measuring rod that allows for differentiation. What Paul warns against in 12:3 is either imposing that norm on others or failing to live up to it oneself. The "sober-mindedness" of Christians is therefore the sober maintenance of the norm that one has been given.

The result is that faith for Paul is not a single dogmatic standard as has traditionally been supposed. The argument of Romans is misunderstood when one takes the theological argument of the first eleven chapters as if they were not integrally connected with the ethic of the last four. Paul's argument as a whole is that faith in Jesus Christ has pluralistic possibilities. There are political, ideological, racial, and temperamental components that are legitimately connected with faith, comprising the peculiar "measuring rod" that each person in the church has been given. The dangers that Paul attempts to ward off in Rom. 12:3 are similar to those faced by earlier Greek theorists: to maintain liberty and personal integrity without falling into either arrogance or nihilism. Although Glenn Tinder does not cite this verse, his view is forged from the same synthesis between the Socratic and the Christian tradition that Paul articulates: "There is no perfect revelation or vision; all faith is conceived in partial darkness. . . . Pride in one's own understanding is an almost unmistakable sign of the inadequacy of that understanding. . . . Religion negates, and does not support, the pride of doctrine which is one of the chief sources of intolerance."[44]

IV

In Rom. 14:22–23, Paul returns to the theme of maintaining the internal standard of faith; both the conservatives and the liberals in Rome are urged to remain true to their convictions. It is a passage that causes traditionally orthodox interpreters some formidable challenges because it seems to restrict faith to the private sphere and makes individual convictions the final arbiters of decision. The usual translation of this provocative passage is as follows:

> [22]The faith that you have, keep between yourself and God; happy is he who has no reason to judge himself for what he approves. [23]But he who has doubts is condemned, if he eats, because he does not act from faith; for whatever does not proceed from faith is sin. (Rom. 14:22–23, RSV)

Taken out of its historical context of the conflicts between the weak and the strong in Rome, the passage seems to offer loopholes that orthodox interpreters strive to fill. The old H. A. W. Meyer commentary warns against the abuse of this passage, "as though it made all accountability dependent only on subjective moral conviction."[45] W. E. Vine finds it necessary to contradict the passage in his explanation: "Right motives never justify wrong actions. What is evil cannot be excused on the ground of good intentions."[46] Sanday and Headlam trace the use and misuse of the final verse in the ethics of Augustine, Chrysostom, and Aquinas and conclude rather defensively that it "is not a general maxim concerning faith."[47] Karl Barth seeks to eliminate the confident subjectivism of the beatitude in v. 22b by commenting: "Yes; but there is a second consideration.—It is a terrible thing to be thus alone with God." Concerning the maxim about sin being whatever does not proceed from faith, Barth queries: "Who then is justified? Who dares to say, 'I have faith'? . . . Who dares to harp upon the theme of his own autonomy?" There is no hint in Barth's brief explanation of Rom. 14:22–23 that it deals with one of the profound pillars of tolerance in Pauline thought.[48]

The interpreter who seems most clearly to grasp the significance of these verses and their connection with "the measuring rod of faith" in Rom. 12:3 is Ernst Käsemann. He observes that just prior to these verses Paul has explained why he agrees with the position of the strong in Rome, that "everything is indeed clean" (14:20), so that one should not have to be bound by cultic regulations. But Paul fears that this may lead the weak members of the church into violating their own more constricted standards. "Paul is warning against a violated conscience and protecting against a straying conscience in order to preserve one's humanity. For him it is undoubtedly sin to force the conscience of another. . . . Sin arises, however, when one goes beyond the gift of God, instead of attending to one's own *metron pisteōs* ["measuring rod of faith"], and thus falls into *huperphronein* ["super-mindedness"]. Faith is a concrete orientation to the lordship of Christ which grasps it, in which its breadth leaves room for the particularities of the members, which does not impose uniformity. . . . No one must make his faith a norm for others as they seek to serve Christ. The weak want uniformity by making their law binding for brothers and sisters, and the strong seek it too by forcing their insight on the weak. We thus try to make others in our own image and in so doing sin, since faith has to do always and exclusively with the image of Christ."[49] The passage clearly implies that each person has a unique norm of faith that should be maintained in integrity. Not only should one keep it intact for oneself, despite commu-

nal pressures to conform, but also one should avoid imposing it on others. Tolerance here rests on the pillar of the
autonomous conscience.

One of the unresolved problems about Rom. 14:22–23 is
that "faith" seems to be used with a different connotation
here than earlier in Romans. Cranfield argues that the term
is used here "in its special sense of confidence that one's
faith allows one to do a particular thing," and he has a
difficult time coordinating this with what he takes to be the
usual connotation of faith in Romans as "belief that something is true."[50] Others suggest that the term "faith" in this
context implies "conviction"[51] or "good conscience."[52]
Even Käsemann concedes that faith implies something like
"persuasion" in these verses. I believe this problem can be
resolved by carrying through with the connection between
these verses and 12:3, where Paul speaks of "the measuring
rod of faith." When Paul urges that faith should be kept
"between yourself and God," this is ordinarily taken as a
demand for privacy[53] or modesty.[54] But the preposition
translated "between" could with equal justification be
translated "according to, in conformity with."[55] This would
produce the meaning: "Keep your faith which you have in
accordance with yourself before God." In other words,
remain true to your "measuring rod." This translation
would allow full consistency in the use of "faith" in
Romans 12–14. Faith is the individual appropriation of
grace that contains elements of ideological and racial iden-
tity. In 14:22–23, Paul is restating the demand for personal
integrity and for respecting the integrity of others.

This view of faith comports well with the unifying purpose of Romans, to find common ground between competing factions of the church in Rome. As Bartsch—among
others—has shown, "faith" is used more frequently as a
term in Romans than in any other Biblical book, and its
apparent purpose is to provide unity between these factions, particularly between Jewish Christians and Gentile
Christians. "This unity is a unity of faith, but a faith which

unites Jews and Christians and not a faith which could make a brother stumble (14:21). Thus, the meaning of the concept 'faith' is important not only dogmatically, but also in regard to the specific purpose of the letter."[56] The irony, of course, is that the misunderstanding of Paul's conception of faith has been so crucial a factor in Christian intolerance. The Thirty Years' War between Catholics and Protestants was fought, in effect, over what appeared to be mutually exclusive ways of understanding (or misunderstanding) faith in Romans. It is only when Paul's argument about the individuation of faith is understood that genuinely tolerant unity is possible.

The result of this new hypothesis[57] is that the final maxim can be taken in a general sense that is consistent with the earlier theological argument of Romans. "Whatever does not proceed from [this individuated] faith is sin," because if one either absolutizes one's faith or abandons it under pressure from others, one falls into the self-imposed wrath described in Rom. 1:18ff. To absolutize faith by imposing it on others is in effect to make oneself into God, to refuse "to honor him as God or give thanks to him" which leads to zealous futility (1:21). But to abandon faith and fall into relativism by adopting the standards of others produces "all manner of wickedness, evil, covetousness, malice . . ." (Rom. 1:28–32). These are precisely the extremes that Paul warns against in Rom. 12:3, bidding his readers "not to be super-minded above what one ought to be minded, but to set your mind on being sober-minded, each according to the measuring rod of faith that God has dealt out." To grasp the connection between individuated faith and social tolerance as they are articulated in these verses is to be led directly into the polar antithesis of the next chapter. If one has faith without tolerance, one attempts to impose one's faith on others; but if one has tolerance without faith, one fails to maintain one's own integrity and falls into relativism and conformity. To pursue the logic of these alternatives will lead us into a central nexus of Pauline theology, the need to preserve the tension between the First and the Second Commandment.

One thing is clear, however, in conclusion: The foundation of tolerance is the individuation of faith. Tolerance requires resistance against the tyranny of dogma, but a resistance of a different sort than enlightenment and liberal skepticism about the legitimacy of dogma itself. Pauline theology allows a maintenance of the limited concerns of ideology. Each person has the obligation to be true to "the measuring rod" that he or she has been given, and, as that norm evolves, to act in accordance with it along the path. To fail to do so, or to fall into the opposite temptation of imposing it on others, is to disregard both Sinai and Delphi.

Chapter III

FAITH WITHOUT TOLERANCE
AND
TOLERANCE WITHOUT FAITH

Faith in Pauline thought is the relation one assumes toward the transcendent Lord. In the epistle to the Romans, in particular, the emblems of transcendence are righteousness, holiness, and glory. When humans assume an arrogant or heedless relation to these emblems, they fall into fanaticism or relativism. Tolerance can be preserved only when a genuinely faithful relation to transcendence is maintained.

The issue of transcendence has played a decisive role since the beginning of the debate over tolerance in the sixteenth century. One of the key arguments in favor of tolerance was worked out by Sebastian Franck, who held that individual mystical experience was the ultimate source of religious knowledge, and that in view of the transcendence of God, no one could claim to have a definitive form of such experience.[1] As Roland Bainton pointed out: "Franck saw paradox everywhere. . . . The whole attempt to formulate a theology in articles was for him an idle performance. He was an extreme disciple of the *ignorantia sacra* ["holy ignorance"]."[2] Although not proceeding from the same mystical tradition, Glenn Tinder's pathbreaking treatise on tolerance stresses much the same point. "I think the key to tolerance lies in thus respecting reason but not overestimating it—in recognizing that it may disclose something of absolute being but cannot provide final and all-embracing knowledge."[3] He insists on the need to stay "open" to "transrational insight," which remains necessarily tentative in its formulation.[4] Tolerance remains a possibility when one adopts a relationship to such transrational insights that avoids fanaticism as well as relativism.

The thesis of this chapter is that Pauline theology offers an approach to transcendence that allows an integration of such insights with the First and Second Commandments. The First Commandment, that one should have no other gods, preserves the relation to transcendence from the dangers of relativism. The Second Commandment, that one should refrain from worshiping graven images, guards the transcendent from idolatrous human depictions and definitions. Tolerance, I shall argue, requires that the tension between these two commandments be preserved. Faith without tolerance violates the Second Commandment, making a graven image out of some finite definition of the transcendent. Tolerance without faith violates the First Commandment, refusing to choose the God who stands transcendent above all lesser realities. Zealous fanaticism thus violates the Second Commandment, while relativism and nihilism violate the First. Healthy tolerance is the social corollary of a faith that retains the discipline of both the First and the Second Commandment. To provide the background for this perspective we begin with a brief account of the role of the First and Second Commandments in the Old Testament.

I

It is generally agreed that the First and Second Commandments constitute a unique feature of Old Testament faith. Werner H. Schmidt has recently summarized the consensus that the ancient Near East provided neither a close analogy nor an actual parallel to the demand of exclusive faith linked with the prohibition of images.[5] A literal translation of the first two commandments in Ex. 20:3–4 is as follows: "There shall not be to you other gods before my face." "You shall not make for yourself any graven image . . ."[6] The first command has to do with the exclusive relationship with Yahweh. It does not deny the existence of "other gods" but simply demands that they not be allowed to intrude in the "face-to-face" relationship between Yahweh and his people. As Jay G. Williams explains: "God also has a face, a presence among men. . . . In experiencing the exodus and in hearing God's voice in the thunder Israel is confronted by God's face and learns, through knowing him, that now she can no longer fear, worship, or believe in other powers. Before his face, that is before those very concrete and observable events which led to Israel's freedom, she must affirm that he is the one and only God."[7] In the early period of Israelite thought, this commandment was not so much an intellectual claim of monotheism as a demand for unconditional loyalty to the God who had redeemed his people. It had to do with faith in its relational rather than its objectifying aspect.

The dimensions of the First Commandment were worked out in several directions, as Schmidt has shown. First, the notion of Yahweh as a "jealous God" was linked with the exclusivity of relationship.[8] Jealousy, or zeal, does not imply envy on Yahweh's part toward other gods, whatever their powers might be, but rather a passionate commitment analogous to monogamous marriage. Second, the claim of Deuteronomy that "the LORD our God is one" (Deut. 6:4) countered both the multiplicity of Canaanite gods and goddesses and the varying branches of early Israel. It later came to imply the unity of ultimate reality and the singularity of truth. In this sense Deuteronomy extends the First Commandment into a principle of absolute monotheism. Third, as Deuteronomy elaborates the doctrine of oneness, it is linked with a demand of totally engrossing loyalty. Samuel Terrien provides a provocative translation of Deut. 6:4–5 that shows the connection between the oneness of God and the singular devotion of human faith: "Hear, O Israel, Yahweh, our Elohim, Yahweh is One. *And* thou shalt love Yahweh thy Elohim with thy whole mind, and with thy whole drive for self-preservation, and with the 'muchness' of thy whole being."[9] The passionate totality of this relationship emulates the zeal of Yahweh, which means that despite the hiddenness and transcendence of the one true God, persons of faith are to give themselves to God as unreservedly as God gives himself to his people. As Schmidt concludes: "In Deuteronomy love toward God means keeping the first commandment."[10]

The Second Commandment deals with the universal human tendency to desire a finite definition of and control over transcendent deity. To grasp what is at stake in "graven images" it is necessary to understand the function of idols in ancient Near Eastern religion. Williams explains that "polytheists recognized that man's life is affected profoundly by the cosmic, social, and subconscious powers of existence. Confronted directly, these powers appear as seemingly uncontrollable and hence frightening urgings and forces. . . . The making of images not only expressed in a visual way the reality of these powers; it also provided, through objectification, a means whereby a person could deal with them. The idols of ancient men were a way of putting existence in order and hence of achieving sanity. By creating idols and images of the deities, men could place these forces at 'arm's length' so that they could be addressed and placated."[11] To place Yahweh on the level of such forces was not only to deny his victory over tyrannical political and religious structures based on polytheism but also to reduce the transcendent to the finite. The powers that polytheists attempted to depict through visual and mythic metaphors were real enough—but their reality was finite. To make such limited realities into objects of worship was to enter into the realm of untruth, and as Israel's experience with polytheism revealed, such untruth always had a tyrannical social corollary. Humans have a way of placing themselves and each other in bondage to such untruths.

The scope of the Second Commandment is much wider than the mere prohibition of visual images. The iconoclastic movements in Christianity and Islam have tended to overlook this scope, which clearly included not only the images they were attacking but also the theological certitudes by which such attacks were justified. Jay G. Williams, once again, states the matter in an effective manner: "Since the second commandment is primarily an attempt to assert the indefinability and incomprehensibility of God in the face of humanity's natural propensity to make idols, it is far more universal in scope than at first meets the eye, . . . for God is beyond any limiting picture or description. Thus the commandment applies just as rigorously to the theologian who makes lofty definitions which claim to delineate God's essence as to the woodcarver or metalworker. The second commandment . . . teaches the indefinability of God."[12] This has a direct bearing on the issue of tolerance, because if truth is finally elusive, there is no justification in requiring others to assent to a particular formulation or depiction. There is a principled basis for intellectual humility in the Second Commandment, one that opens the human community to an ongoing quest for adequate, though never final, formulations of the truth. If one had the Second Commandment without the First, however, the severity of such an aniconic faith would quickly drift into despair and nihilism.

There is a very real sense in which the First and Second Commandments are two connected sides of the same coin. This is certainly the case as far as the Old Testament evidence is concerned. Schmidt reminds us "that the Old Testament in many ways views the first and second commandments as a unity."[13] This view of their unity is manifest in the words of explanation "for I, Yahweh, am a zealous God," which pertain to the First as well as the Second Commandment (Ex. 20:3–6; Deut. 5:7–10). It is reflected in prophetic material like Isa. 40:18: "To whom then will you liken God, or what likeness compare with him?" It is expressed in hymnic material like Ps. 89:6: "For

who in the skies can be compared to the LORD? Who among
the heavenly beings is like the LORD?" The exclusive
relationship with this incomparable God is called faith; but
if faith rests only in the First Commandment, it becomes
fanatical, incapable of grasping the limitation of its knowledge of the God who stands above all the gods, even the
gods of religious law, custom, and theology. The two
commandments stand in perennial tension with each other,
the guardians of genuine faith. To give up the First Commandment is to fall into relativism and malaise, while to
eliminate the Second is to end up in zealotism. It is only
when the tension between the First and the Second Commandment is preserved and celebrated that faith results in
tolerance. Moreover, I would assert, it is only when this
tension is preserved that tolerance itself remains healthy.

II

We turn next to Paul's argument in Romans where the
Scylla of fanaticism and the Charybdis of relativism are
analyzed. These two extremes of unfaith are related, it
seems to me, to a betrayal of the Second and First Commandments. Although both are alluded to in Rom. 1:21–25,
it is the violation of the First Commandment that seems
uppermost in Paul's argument at the beginning of the letter.

In Rom. 1:18–32, Paul generalizes on the typical sins of
the Gentiles, as seen from the perspective of Jewish missionary propaganda, and succeeds in including all humans
in the indictment. As Cranfield concludes: "We understand
these verses as the revelation of the gospel's judgment of all
men, which lays bare not only the idolatry of ancient and
modern paganism but also the idolatry ensconced in Israel,
in the Church, and in the life of each believer."[14] The
passage is particularly interesting because it shows not only
the source of "tolerance without faith" but also its consequences. Several distinctive features of social disorder are
visible in this passage. It falls under three general head-

ings: relativism, intellectual futility, and anomie, or norm-lessness. I begin with the first of these themes.

A. *The Shape of Moral Relativism.* Intellectual and moral relativism are particularly touched on in Rom. 1:18 and 32, at the beginning and end of the opening argument of Romans. Romans 1:18 sets the theme of the entire discussion, declaring the wrath of God as a historical reality acting against the "unrighteousness" of humans who "suppress the truth." As Käsemann and others have argued, the reference to "ungodliness and unrighteousness" in this verse is not to the first and second table of the laws, the religious and the ethical, but to the totality of human rebellion.[15] Rather than allowing truth to stand, we replace it with our smaller truths, and in effect allow our own "unrighteousness" to be the last word. Paul spells this out by arguing in subsequent verses that the truth of God's creative order and justice is manifest to everyone, but that humans refuse to acknowledge it as such (Rom. 1:20–25).

Although exegetes have tended to view this as an argument against idolatry, I think it fits much more closely the situation of relativism that was characteristic of the Greco-Roman world. Paul speaks not of committing oneself to a single lie, or even of denying the truth, but rather of suppressing the truth. He speaks in Rom. 1:21 of persons "knowing God" but refusing to glorify him as God, that is, refusing to give God first place. It is a matter of reducing truth to the same level as everything else, which ends up placing subjective preferences in the final place of authority.

Greco-Roman relativism is visible in the popular philosophical movements. The Cynics, Stoics, and Epicureans did not deny the reality of the various religious traditions of the ancient world; they simply relativized them by the concept of the pantheon, in which the gods of various city-states were essentially on a level with each other, each laying claim to only a fraction of the truth. Although the Stoics emphasized the single truth of the *logos* that lies behind all these partial truths, the others tended to be more devoted to the task of iconoclasm, of breaking down the claims of the various religious traditions.

The moral relativism that resulted from this intellectual stance is summarized in Rom. 1:32: "They know God's righteous decree that those who practice such things deserve death; yet they not only do them but actually applaud others who practice them." Earlier exegetes, especially the church fathers, devoted a good deal of attention to the question of whether it was really correct to say that those who approve of evil deeds are as guilty as those who do them.[16] Paul's interest in this verse appears to lie elsewhere, namely, in describing the encouragement to license that moral and intellectual relativism provided. If all truth is relative, and if no norm is valid, then the enlightened person will show an advanced state of development by violating them. Sophistication is then proven by the courage to wreck the norms.

C. H. Dodd has pointed out the allusions to relativism in Rom. 1:32: "This precisely hits off the fatal ambiguity of the moral judgment of Graeco-Roman civilization. That the ordinary man of the time had a bad conscience about such practices is hardly doubtful, and the maxim of Stoicism, that what is 'contrary to nature' is evil, was widely accepted. But public opinion acquiesced in, condoned, or even, as Paul says, applauded practices which it often surrounded with an unwholesome sentimentality."[17] Probably Dodd had in mind practices such as pederasty, which was being gilded with sentimentality during Paul's time, while in the view of traditional moralists it was considered a disgrace. A broad chorus of voices has recently depicted the scope of a similar relativism among American intellectuals. Meg Greenfield writes that political discussion is paralyzed by the sense that "old certainties keep crashing down. . . . In the good old days, the foundations of belief took a lot longer to crumble—or at least enough longer to spare the average person the jeers and taunts of the crowd."[18]

Peter Shaw describes the "degenerate criticism" that is becoming more and more popular in the field of English studies in American universities. "Certainty and piety of all kinds are systematically undermined in favor of a universal relativism of values and judgment."[19] He goes on to describe, for example, the current trend in the field of Elizabethan and Jacobean literature to deny that a play or a poem means what it appears to mean. "In one article after another in the most prestigious academic journals the shared experience of audiences and readers for some 300 years are regularly overthrown."[20] Shaw sees the widespread tendency toward "the devaluation of values" as an expression of a wider phenomenon: "the erosion of certainty about what is true and right." Literature students learn from their professors that such erosion is truly critical and avantgarde: "Academic criticism starts with the assumption that there are no such things as admirable human beings, unequivocally admirable acts, or truly pure motives for acts. To prove that these do not exist, every conceivable method of questioning motives is employed. . . . The assumption is taught that the end justifies the means."[21]

John Gardner's book *On Moral Fiction* seeks to counter such trends and to insist on the traditional view "that true art is moral: it seeks to improve life, not debase it. It seeks to hold off, at least for a while, the twilight of the gods and us. . . . Art asserts and reasserts those values which hold off dissolution, struggling to keep the mind intact and preserve the city, the mind's safe preserve. Art rediscovers, generation by generation, what is necessary to humanness. Criticism restates and clarifies, reinforces the wall."[22] He charges that in abandoning these traditional tasks, modern literature and films present "escapist models or else moral evasiveness, or, worse, cynical attacks on traditional values such as honesty, love of country, marital fidelity, work, and moral courage. This is not to imply that such values are absolutes, too holy to attack. But it is dangerous to raise a generation that smiles at such values, or has never heard of them, or dismisses them with indignation, as if they were not relative goods but were absolute evils."[23] Alexander Solzhenitsyn has argued that the trend toward relativism is, in effect, due to the loss of respect for the First Commandment. He writes: "On the way from the Renaissance to our days, we have enriched our experience, but we have lost the concept of a Supreme Complete Entity which used to restrain our passions and our irresponsibility. . . . This is the real crisis."[24] In Solzhenitsyn's case, unfortunately, the requirements of the First Commandment are not matched by a sensitivity to the Second, which leads to an absolutizing of his own position and a repudiation of the ideals of an open society. A more adequate balance between the two commandments that results in a systematic defense of tolerance is available in Romans. Solzhenitsyn is in agreement with Paul, however, on the question of the ultimate root of relativism.

B. *The Theological Root of Relativism.* A great deal of debate has centered on whether Paul falls into a "natural theology" in Rom. 1:18ff., and the similarities as well as differences from Hellenistic Judaism have been thereby brought to the light. I agree with Käsemann that Paul radicalizes the typical Jewish apologetic in this section, seeing the sin of paganism not in lack of knowledge but in rebellion against the recognized God of all creation. This radicalization is guided by a commitment to the First Commandment, in Käsemann's view: "According to our text the wrath of God descends as a curse from Heaven onto those who reject the first commandment."[25] Käsemann has v. 21 particularly in view at this point: "Though they have known God, they have not glorified him as God or given him thanks, but have become futile in their reasons." The same theme is driven home in v. 25: "They have actually exchanged the truth of God for the lie, and worshiped and served the creature instead of the Creator." The essence of sin, according to this passage, is placing the ultimate truth on the same level as all other truths, which in the final analysis results in allowing personal preference to be the final arbiter of truth.

As Käsemann and others have suggested, Paul is here viewing the entire realm of pagan religion under the rubric of the golden calf episode. It offers a possibility of seeing idolatry essentially as a projection mechanism, in which the self and its needs become the center of worship. To worship the "creature" in the form of a symbol of human desires for prosperity and sexual gratification—the meaning of the golden calf—is really to worship oneself. And just as in the episode in Exodus, such worship leads almost immediately to moral chaos—the orgy, in which everyone's desire for gratification, having been raised to the ultimate degree, is to be satisfied without qualms (Ex. 32:6–7, 18–19). When one refuses to give final loyalty to the transcendent truth, the desires of the creature take its place. When that happens, all else disintegrates. As the poet Yeats wrote a generation ago: "Things fall apart; the center cannot hold; Mere anarchy is loosed upon the world."

At the root of this collapse, for Paul, lies the refusal to "glorify God as God" and to "give thanks" (Rom. 1:21). This is the response of worship, the acknowledgment of the ultimate, which, though beyond our perfect definition, is nevertheless worthy of our devotion. God is the source of all our blessings. Worship in this sense is the proper exercise of the First Commandment: acknowledging the reality of other truths, but allowing none of them to come "before his face." The personal result of this stance, as Käsemann, Ebeling, and many others have stressed in the past generation, is to place humans in their rightful place, as finite and dependent creatures. In this sense, the First Commandment is the chief guardian of genuine humanity, a hedge against persons becoming arrogant enough to think they are gods, which, if the Garden of Eden story be taken in its full theological depth, is the perennial story of the fall of the race (cf. Gen. 3:5).

The constant danger of tolerance without faith is that it

falls into such relativistic malaise, encouraging the raising of personal preference to the point of ultimate concern. When this happens, the social fabric rips, and no limits are left. Social chaos is the long-term result, and tolerance itself is an inevitable casualty.

C. *The Consequences of Relativism.* In the complex flow of the argument in Rom. 1:18–32 there are several references to intellectual futility as a distinctive indication of refusing to honor God in accordance with the First Commandment. Paul lays down the premise of natural revelation that the best of the Greek philosophers in his day would have accepted, that God's "invisible nature, namely, his eternal power and deity, has been clearly perceived in the things that have been made" (Rom. 1:20). Rather than acknowledging such deity, however, humans "suppress the truth" (1:18) through relativism, with the result that their very capacity to discern reality is impaired: "They were made empty in their thinking and their senseless heart was darkened" (1:21; translation mine). Both reason and emotion are thus corrupted and rendered futile. Commentators are clear that Paul has in mind a "loss of touch with reality";[26] but only rarely is the connection with repudiating the truth of the First Commandment explained. Ernst Käsemann comes the closest to catching the basic idea: Paul refers to emptiness or vanity "as the characteristic of the world which breaks free from its creatureliness and which God in his wrath delivers up to itself. Since mention had just been made of idolatry, the verb probably reflected the Old Testament characterizing of idols as vain. He who disregards the truth falls . . . into the futility caused thereby, and into the related darkness. He becomes incapable of discriminating perception, loses any grasp of reality, and falls victim of illusion."[27]

I believe that reflection on the consequences of moral relativism can bring the Pauline stress on intellectual futility even more sharply into focus. Far from making unfair and sweeping allegations about Greco-Roman culture,[28] Paul lays hold of an underlying tendency that proceeds with inexorable intellectual and emotional force. If the ultimate truth is unavailable and every human approximation is questioned with equal vigor, the courage to continue the intellectual quest is fatally impaired. The mind and heart cannot be compelled to continue long in hopeless pursuits. The result is despair concerning the potential of either the rational mind or the human emotions. A person or a culture caught in such despair exhibits the kind of emptiness and darkness that Paul describes in Rom. 1:21b—a mind that refuses to come to grips with constantly elusive objects of knowledge, and a heart that refuses to abide by its human impulses because they no longer appear more appropriate than the basest desires.

The connection between intellectual and emotional futility and the loss of a commitment to the ultimate truth is more clearly alluded to by critics of the current cultural scene than by most of the commentators on the epistle to the Romans. Peter Shaw describes the intellectual paralysis that has emerged in the wake of deconstructivism and revisionism in literary criticism: "What is being claimed for the first time . . . is that we must give up any illusion that we can gain a clear understanding of the written word. The paradoxes of communication, formerly regarded as challenges to the wits of writer and reader, are now considered primary, absolute bars to any degree of certainty whatsoever. . . . The issue compromising academic criticism today is simply whether it is possible to mean what one says and to convey that meaning to others. Anyone wishing to answer in the affirmative must begin by confronting the new language of indeterminism."[29]

An even more striking expression of "empty" and "darkened" intellectual and emotional powers is found in Benjamin DeMott's review of John Barth's novel *Letters*. The novel depicts the creation of a film whose theme is "the destruction of the universe of language. During its shooting, the author, scriptwriter, and director scrap hilariously for aesthetic control. Part of the action portrays antiverbalist cabals led by persons from Barth's books waging war on each other to determine who is to dominate the nonverbal arts of the future. And the impresario at the helm [is] a ferociously word-hating monster named Reg Prinz," who selects as the climax of his film the sacking of Washington's historical archives with the intention of destroying "the venerable metropolis of letters."[30] Not only does the book repudiate the world of language by which the human mind describes and copes with reality; it also invites readers to contemplate the resultant mayhem without the slightest moral revulsion. Just as Paul saw a parallel decline in the powers of both the "mind" and the "heart," so DeMott describes the world that Barth has created in this and other novels: "There is something in this late-twentieth-century embrace of the theme of reality as mirage that hints at enfeebled responsiveness—inability to awaken any sense of pain and injustice except that which deals abstractly with them as 'clichés.' "[31] The political embodiment of such a "darkened" and unresponsive condition of the heart was painfully manifest in the reply of a recent Secretary of State to the question of complicity in the genocidal disaster in Cambodia: "Who gives a damn?"[32] If all truth is mere mirage, then any atrocity can be condoned. It is not only a world of meaningful language that is endangered; rather, the world itself is endangered.

Disregarding such dangers, the tendency toward self-assertion in such a relativistic environment is trenchantly described by Paul in the following verse: "claiming to be wise, they were made foolish" (Rom. 1:22; translation mine). The word translated with "claiming" implies "boastful, ardent assertion,"[33] lacking evidence or support beyond the voice of the claimant. In a vivid manner Franz Leenhardt describes the process of self-worship alluded to in this verse: "Thus, in refusing God, men still make for themselves a god suggested by their darkened minds. . . . Thus 'religion' is born, springing from a rejected knowledge of the true God and finalizing man's seizure of God, the triumphs of gods over God."[34] Here we encounter the disorder of self-identity that typically arises in a relativistic age. When the countervailing forces of custom, traditional certitude, and external authority disappear, all the self has left is bare self-assertion. The "good, the true, and the beautiful" are whatever I wish them to be at any given moment. Peter Shaw describes the familiar effect of this tendency in college and university literature classes: "Just as the revisionists are led to reduce the act of criticism to a given critic's subjective preference, so do professors relegate judgement of all sorts to the students' subjective preferences."[35] In such a situation humans truly become the measure of all things. The pride against which the Greek tragedians and the Biblical wisdom warned becomes routine.

The rankest absurdities follow, as Paul sketches four of what his readers would have considered the silliest forms of Greco-Roman idolatry, in which people "exchanged the glory of the immortal God for images resembling mortal man or birds or animals or reptiles" (Rom. 1:23). Hellenistic philosophers as well as Jewish propagandists had ridiculed such remnants of archaic nature worship, so Paul was in one sense not breaking any new ground in this formulation. But he clearly has in view the irrational consequences of thoroughgoing relativism: When the compass needle of truth points in all directions at once, the most absurd and archaic ideologies and superstitions crowd back to the surface. There no longer remains a basis to distinguish the reasonable from the irrational, the healthy from the unhealthy. If there is no single God and no genuine form of truth available to humans, then why not worship snakes and emulate their inhuman values?

The moral consequences of relativism are described in Rom. 1:24–32. The depiction of moral perversion in v. 24 and the subsequent elucidation in vs. 26–31 add up to an appalling state of anomie:

Therefore God gave them up in the lusts of their hearts to
impurity, to the dishonoring of their bodies among themselves.... Their women exchanged natural relations for
unnatural.... God gave them up to a base mind and to
improper conduct. They were filled with all manner of
wickedness, evil, covetousness, malice. Full of envy, murder, strife, deceit, malignity, they are gossips, slanderers,
haters of God, insolent, haughty, boastful, inventors of evil,
disobedient to parents, foolish, faithless, heartless, ruthless.

Beginning with what may have seemed to some of Paul's
Greco-Roman congregation as a relatively harmless preference for sexual perversion, fueled by the pleasure of
wrecking traditional norms, one ends up engulfed in the
most murderous passions. Commentators and preachers
have often been so concerned to draw moralistic implications from these verses that the connection between norm-
lessness and the loss of the First Commandment is overlooked. But Paul reiterates his point in the very center of
the depiction, in v. 25: "... because they exchanged the
truth about God for a lie and worshiped and served the
creature rather than the Creator, who is blessed forever!
Amen." These sins are not the cause of wrath, but the
expression of it. As Käsemann points out, it was the traditional view of Hellenistic Judaism that godlessness is the
source of all evil, "but Paul paradoxically reverses the
cause and consequence: Moral perversion is the result of
God's wrath, not the reason for it."[36]

The effort to discern a logical development within the
catalog of vices has proved fruitless, except that the series
begins with four terms with rhymed endings, and the series
ends with four terms beginning with a-, nicely rendered in
a parallel fashion in the RSV: "foolish, faithless, heartless,
ruthless."[37] It is as if the vices spring out in random order,
"in rapid succession as from Pandora's box," conveying a
sense that "idolatry opens the floodgates for vices which
destroy society and turn creation back into terrible chaos."[38] Normlessness eliminates the last vestiges of order,

allowing the darkness to triumph over the world. What Paul describes here is an extreme form of the "mass disintegration" that Glenn Tinder perceives as the distinctive feature of twentieth-century social life, "a sundering of man from nature, from place, from possessions, from fellow man, and finally from himself." It is not so much a separation of humans from the values that they wish to pursue as "a kind of primal separation in which there are no known or attainable values. The mood is often one of an elemental and damning detachment. It is not hard to call a roll of authors who have described this emotion: Franz Kafka, F. Scott Fitzgerald, Sherwood Anderson, Ernest Hemingway, Jean-Paul Sartre, Henry Miller, Alberto Moravia, J. D. Salinger."[39] The excruciating pain of such a situation has been carefully described by the psychological and sociological studies of anomie.[40]

Of particular significance for our reflections on the problem of tolerance are the studies of the impact of modern pluralism, which contribute to this widespread sense of anomie. In *The Homeless Mind*, Peter Berger describes the result of tolerant pluralism eroding the final vestiges of religious certainty:

> The "homelessness" of modern social life has found its most devastating expression in the area of religion. The general uncertainty, both cognitive and normative, brought about by the pluralization of everyday life and of biography in modern society, has brought religion into a serious crisis of plausibility. The age-old function of religion—to provide ultimate certainty amid the exigencies of the human condition—has been severely shaken. Because of the religious crisis in modern society, social "homelessness" has become metaphysical—that is, it has been "homelessness" in the cosmos. This is very difficult to bear.[41]

I believe that the similarities between these modern trends and the situation in first-century culture account in part for the stunning prescience of Paul's analysis. He addresses the issue of relativism and its consequences at a theological level that makes Romans perennially relevant. Tolerance without faith is a curse whose burden is excruciating, because God gives us up to the very moral and intellectual chaos that our denial of the First Commandment entails.

III

When we search through Romans for references to the violation of the Second Commandment, connections with the opposite danger to relativism are not explicitly developed (Rom. 1:23; 2:22). All I would want to claim is that the problems of religious pride and zealous fanaticism are dealt with in a manner in which a connection with a loss of the Second Commandment can be supplied. Faith without tolerance tends to absolutize itself and fall thereby into pride that presumes on the grace of God and into zeal that ends up opposing God.

The first of these alternatives is lifted up in Paul's description of the sins of boasting and hypocrisy that afflict the legalistic proponents of Judaism. When one reads these lines, the inflated rhetoric betrays a boasting spirit that is the antithesis of genuine Jewish faith:

> [17]But if you call yourself a Jew and rely upon the law and boast of your relation to God [18]and know his will and approve what is excellent, because you are instructed in the law, [19]and if you are sure that you are a guide to the blind, a light to those who are in darkness, [20]a corrector of the foolish, a teacher of children, having in the law the embodiment of knowledge and truth . . . (Rom. 2:17–20)

As the commentators have shown, all the honorific terms in this passage were occasionally used in Jewish mission propaganda, but never with such arrogance as here. Otto Michel catches the faint tone of sarcasm as Paul describes how "the teacher of the law looks down beneficently and patronizingly as an 'educator' upon 'fools,' as a 'teacher' upon 'children.' "[42] James Moffatt refers to this depiction of

"an overweening pride in his religious privileges and a
contempt for 'lesser breeds without the law.' "[43] Early
Christian readers could hardly have missed the allusions to
Jesus' criticism of the Pharisees as blind leaders of the
blind (Matt. 23:16) and as boasters in the Temple that they
were better than sinful tax collectors (Luke 18:11).[44] Perhaps the outrageous quality of such boastful behavior is in
part responsible for Paul's leaving the sentence incom-
plete. In one sense the completion should be supplied by
any perceptive reader, i.e.: "If you 'boast in God' in this
manner, you violate the very relation with him in the
process; such boasting is hypocrisy itself."

This unspoken issue of hypocrisy is driven home in the
five rhetorical questions in vs. 21–23:

> You then who teach others, will you not teach yourself?
> While you preach against stealing, do you steal? You who
> say that one must not commit adultery, do you commit
> adultery? You who abhor idols, do you rob temples? You
> who boast in the law, do you dishonor God by breaking the
> law? (Rom. 2:21–23)

Despite the fact that most observant Jews in the first
century had a robust conscience, and were not aware of
overt violations of the law, there were some rather notorious loopholes that Paul exploits in these questions. There
were ways to steal and commit adultery by shrewd uses of
the law. The matter of robbing pagan temples could be
justified—despite the Eighth Commandment and the explicit prohibition of Deut. 7:25—on the grounds that it was
good to thwart idolatry. According to yet another Rabbinic
rationalization, since the owner of the temple was a pagan
god who did not exist anyway, the property could be
considered ownerless.[45] But Paul leaves no space for clever
casuistry, driving home the final question about those who
boast the loudest about instructing babes to respect the
Torah and then violate it themselves (Rom. 2:23). The effect
of these questions following the uncompleted sentence of

boasting was almost irresistible, in Käsemann's view: "The advantages of the Jew are impressively accumulated, and then when they reach their crest they break to pieces like a wave. Similarly the harsh and sharp accusations in the brief questions in vs. 21–22 are like a barrage that completely traps the one who is addressed. Stylistically the discrepancy between claim and performance could hardly be more impressively emphasized."[46]

The issue of boasting that is touched with such irony in the passages just cited is developed into a basic theological doctrine in 3:27ff. Paul has shown that all humans sin, but that God extends grace to everyone through Christ; therefore salvation is a matter of sheer gift and all boasting is controverted:

> [27]Then what becomes of our boasting? It is excluded. On what principle? On the principle of works? No, but on the principle of faith. [28]For we hold that a man is justified by faith apart from works of law. [29]Or is God the God of Jews only? Is he not the God of Gentiles also? Yes, of Gentiles also, [30]since God is one. (Rom. 3:27–30a)

To boast of privileges or superior status is seen here to violate the purposes of God as revealed in the Christ event. It is a denial of the oneness of God, the basic Jewish confession derived, as we have seen, from the First and Second Commandments. To ascribe to weak and sinful creatures the powers that are present only in God is idolatrous. Once again, it is Käsemann who seems to have the sharpest eye for these implications: "Faith and self-boasting are incompatible, for the believer no longer lives out of or for himself.... The monotheistic confession shatters a conception of the law which makes salvation a privilege of the religious. As Creator and Judge God is also the God of the Gentiles and therefore the salvation of the ungodly. As merely the God of the Jews he would cease to be the only God. The full force of this revolutionary statement is seldom perceived."[47] In effect, Paul's argument reveals the "graven image" quality of any boast in human prowess. He thereby creates a systematic hedge against the kind of intolerance that comes from vaunting the superiority of one creed over another.

Paul returns to the issue of faith without tolerance in Rom. 10:1–13, using the technical terms of the religious fanatics who had plagued his ministry and would ultimately be responsible for his imprisonment and death. When Paul writes that his fellow Jews "have a zeal for God, but it is not enlightened" (10:2), the central element in zealous ideology springs into view. Martin Hengel has described the tradition of zealotism that admired the avenger Phinehas (Numbers 25) as the ideal model of faith. It provided the rationale for the terrorist campaigns in Judea and Galilee aimed at eliminating Roman rule and purifying the land of all Gentile influences.[48] Paul's long experience with this ideology of "zeal for God" (which could also be translated "zeal of God") included membership in the wing of the Pharisee movement that favored absolutely uncompromising zeal for the law and violent persecution of lawless elements such as the early Christians (Phil. 3:5–6). After his conversion, Paul found himself a target of this same kind of zealous fanaticism on numerous occasions. At the very time of writing Romans, Paul is concerned about being spared from the violence of "unbelievers in Judea" (Rom. 15:31) when he delivers the offering to Jerusalem. He has already been forced to postpone his departure a considerable length of time after discovering an assassination plot by zealous Jews who have apparently discovered his travel plans (Acts 20:3).

Paul does not question the sincerity of the intolerant zeal of his fellow Jews in Rom. 10:2. Cranfield accurately describes the implication of Paul's choice of words: "Their zeal is zeal for God. . . . Israel is absolutely right in the object of its zeal. And it is undoubtedly zeal—fervent, strenuous, tenacious, concentrated zeal."[49] The problem was that such faith, though fanatical, was "without knowledge" in the sense that it refused to accept the limitation of its view of God's nature and will. This Paul could say from his own personal experience, as one who had been so certain that his view of the law was absolute and that those who thwarted it deserved to die. Paul defines the nature of this missing "knowledge" with a powerful statement that summarizes the central thesis of Romans:

> For, being ignorant of the righteousness that comes from God, and seeking to establish their own, they did not submit to God's righteousness. For Christ is the end of the law, that every one who has faith may be justified. (Rom. 10:3–4)

By absolutizing their own righteousness under the law, the zealous Jews of Paul's time fell into the trap of self-righteousness and found themselves opposing God, whose righteous will was revealed in the tolerant love of Christ. Law as a means of salvation came to an end with Christ, who conveyed the unconditional grace of God, so that those who continue in the tradition of fanatical zeal are doing the very opposite of what they intend. Presuming that they alone were truly submitting to the will of God, they "did not submit to God's righteousness" when it was revealed in the flesh.

A long tradition of Protestant reflection on the issue of this and similar passages has made the problem of salvation by legal conformity very clear. Luther grasped Paul's message with unparalleled clarity: that works righteousness leads to violent opposition to God, while justification by grace alone leads to meekness, love, and tolerance. His words on this issue in the 1531 Lectures on Galatians have a clear relevance for the passage in Romans. Luther identified the Catholic and Anabaptist "fanatics" of his time with the zealots of Paul's day, placing the issue of fanatical zeal on the side of legalism while faith stands on the side of "grace alone." He wrote:

> The doctrine of the fanatics today is the same as that of the false apostles at that time. "If you want to live to God," they

say, "that is, to be alive in the sight of God, then live to the Law, or according to the Law." But we say in opposition: "If you want to live to God, you must completely die to the Law." Human reason and wisdom do not understand this doctrine. Therefore they always teach the opposite.[50]

The problem is that identifying one's ideological opponents as the "fanatics," similar to the zealots whom Paul opposed, overlooks the universal scope of the argument in which Rom. 10:1–13 stands. All, including the most rigorous Protestant, tend to identify their own zeal with the zeal of God, to seek to establish their own righteousness. One person may do so by conformity to law, but another is in the same dilemma by conformity to creed. Paul insists once again a few verses later in Romans 10 that "there is no distinction between Jew and Greek; the same Lord is Lord of all and bestows his riches upon all who call upon him" (Rom. 10:12). This reaffirms the point, developed earlier in Romans, that there is no distinction between humans because all "have sinned and fall short of the glory of God" (Rom. 3:24). Whether Jew or Gentile, conservative or liberal, weak or strong, everyone tends to make a graven image of some particular definition or code, and whenever this occurs, God is opposed and his will is thwarted. Faith without tolerance is just as much a violation of what it means to be truly religious as tolerance without faith.

The dilemma of "zeal without knowledge" was eloquently stated by Jacob Bronowski in an article detailing the implications of twentieth-century physics and mathematics. The more precise the instruments of measurement that scientists devise, the more "fuzzy" and "uncertain" their knowledge seems to become. Bronowski prefers to call Heisenberg's "principle of uncertainty" the "principle of tolerance." He explains: "All knowledge, all information between human beings, can be exchanged only within a play of tolerance. And that is true whether the exchange is in science, or in literature, or in religion, or in politics, or even in any form of thought that aspires to dogma."[51] In a truly memorable passage, Bronowski insists: "There is no absolute knowledge. And those who claim it, whether they are scientists or dogmatists, open the door to tragedy. All information is imperfect. We have to treat it with humility. That is the human condition, and that is what quantum physics says. I mean that literally."[52] Although Paul's evidence was in a completely different arena of human experience, it seems to me that his argument about the dilemma of "zeal without knowledge" comes out at the same place. Its premise is that all humans "see through a glass, darkly" and know only "in part" (I Cor. 13:12).

Not only the tragic conclusion of Paul's own life but also the tragic history of the twentieth century is closely related to faith without tolerance. When Bronowski surveyed the concentration camp and crematorium at Auschwitz, he wrote: "It was done by arrogance. It was done by dogma. It was done by ignorance. When people believe that they have absolute knowledge, with no test in reality, that is how they behave. That is what men do when they aspire to the knowledge of gods."[53] Faith without tolerance indeed seeks to turn believers into gods by absolutizing the content of their belief. The commandment about graven images was designed for the sake of humanity, to ward off the disastrous confusions between mortals and the ultimate truth. But as we have seen in the course of this chapter, avoidance of graven images is not enough. We need a fusion of faith and the principle of uncertainty. The two commandments belong together, the First calling us to the Truth that stands above all truths, and the Second warning us never to assume that our grasp of Truth is final. It is out of this ongoing tension that genuine humanity emerges and that genuine tolerance results.

Chapter IV

THE LIMITS OF TOLERANCE

One of the major dilemmas of tolerance in our time is that it seems to demand the abandonment of limits. In commenting on the nasty impoliteness of a current tennis star, Lance Morrow sadly concludes: "What once would have been intolerable and impermissible public conduct now has become commonplace. If it is not exactly accepted, then at least it is abjectly and wearily endured. Social habit in the United States has taken decisive turns toward the awful. ... Somehow, Americans also have misplaced the moral confidence with which to condemn sleaziness and stupidity. It is as if something in the American judgment snapped, and has remained so long unrepaired that no one notices anymore."[1] The tradition of tolerance based on liberal assumptions lies at the root of this dilemma, and it is not so much a matter of having "snapped" as of having finally produced its inexorable product. If one must be tolerant of others simply out of respect for their individual expressions, it has seemed appropriate to set no limits at all.

The dilemma of limitless tolerance was experienced in acute form in the tragedy of Jim Jones's Peoples Temple in Guyana. Tolerated despite its excesses both in this country and abroad on grounds of the separation of church and state, the cult group moved toward an awful climax of suicidal religious zeal. Sensitive critics like Norman Cousins wrote about "The Reign of the Religious Fanatic," decrying the "mindless assumption in American society that anything calling itself a religion is deserving of special respect and privilege. We apply the term *religious tolerance* indiscriminately and promiscuously, laying ourselves wide open for any charlatan who uses the mumbo-jumbo of 'religion' to accomplish his fraudulent and anti-social designs."[2] Although Cousins can only suggest the measure of denying tax privileges to questionable sects, which would obviously raise horrendous constitutional issues, the problem is a real one. No advocate of tolerance can avoid the question of limits. The current ascendancy of the "Moral Majority" draws a substantial proportion of its strength from precisely this requirement. Its advocates may not provide coherent defense of tolerance, but they are very clear on what its limits ought to be.

One reason why Pauline theology provides so helpful a resource in thinking through the issue of tolerance is that it not only contains a fundamental rationale for its integration with faith but also that it faces the issue of limits in so provocative a manner. A single verse in Romans summarizes the Pauline view that one can detect in every other letter: "[Let] love be genuine, abhorring the evil, cleaving to the good" (Rom. 12:9; translation mine). I will analyze this verse, showing its relation to Paul's stance in general as well as its potential bearing on the current dilemma.

I

The exhortation "Let love be genuine," in Rom. 12:9, comes at the beginning of a series of moral guidelines that ends at Rom. 12:21. Although some exegetes have maintained that these exhortations are "loosely connected" to each other and to the argument of Romans as a whole,[3] I would argue that they were carefully selected and formulated to provide what Paul perceived to be the peculiar needs of the Roman Christians. The question about how love is to be embodied in authentic form serves the larger purpose of

Paul's argument for the ideological autonomy and the mutual respect between competing house churches in Rome. Verse 9 itself is constructed in such a way that when the imperative is understood,[4] the subsequent participial phrases about good and evil detail how the genuineness of love is to be preserved. As Godet writes: "It follows from this construction that . . . 'abhorring, cleaving,' are intended to qualify the love unfeigned. . . . Destitute of this moral rectitude, which is the spirit of holiness, love is only a form of selfishness."[5]

It is interesting to observe that Paul does not exhort the Roman Christians to love. Rather, he presupposes that love is present. It was presumably so natural an expression of the faith that its presence was guaranteed as part of the "gifts" marking all members of the "one body in Christ" (Rom. 12:5–6). Earlier in Romans, Paul referred to the love of God poured into the heart of each Christian (5:5), so that an appropriate appellation for such persons was "beloved" (1:7). His argument had made clear that divine love is completely inclusive and nondiscriminating. It comes to those who least deserve it, regardless of their conformity to the law. It is the tolerant virtue, par excellence.

It therefore seems contradictory to demand that love be "genuine." If the love of God is expressed to evil and good alike, his rain falling on the "just and unjust" as Jesus declared (Matt. 5:45), what business do his disciples have in making discriminations? How can one legitimately place limits on that which is essentially limitless?

A clue to Paul's intention is provided in the only other passage where the word "genuine" is attached to "love." In II Corinthians 6, Paul is summarizing the defense of his apostolic methods in contrast to the attacks by "divine man" missionaries who had invaded Corinth.[6] They boasted of their charismatic abilities, their powerful, even overbearing personalities, and their authority as demonstrated by letters of authentication from other churches and early Christian authorities. Claiming to stand in a succession of "divine men" that ran from Moses through Jesus and Stephen to their own circle, they demanded acknowledgment of their superiority and challenged Paul's authority on the grounds that he did not demonstrate the requisite powers to overcome resistance and ill fortune. In Paul's opinion, these competitive missionaries misused their charismatic gifts—such as love—for the exercise of power and status, claiming to transcend normal ethical standards and the collective judgment of the congregation. His reiteration of the characteristics of authentic ministry is set against this foil:

> As servants of God we commend ourselves in every way: through great endurance, in afflictions, hardships, calamities, beatings, imprisonments, tumults, labors, watching, hunger; by purity, knowledge, forbearance, kindness, the Holy Spirit, *genuine love,* truthful speech, and the power of God . . . (II Cor. 6:4–7)

Even love—as Paul had discovered in the bitter conflict with the "divine man" missionaries—can become exploitative. It can mask the desire to dominate others. It can be reduced to mere sentimentality while more powerful motivations are at work, enslaving and using the subordinate members of a community. It can produce a form of tolerance that allows totalitarian impulses to win the day, fatally crippling the will to maintain the integrity of personal and communal standards. Cranfield captures an aspect of this without referring to the threatening missionaries, noting that Paul "was aware of the danger in this connexion of deceit and—even more serious—of self-deceit, a danger of which the modern champions of 'Not law but love' seem often to be unaware."[7]

When Paul uses the term "genuine" in connection with love, he has communal discussion and controls in mind.[8] Although he develops a series of guidelines in the verses that follow, Paul refrains from attempting to provide a final definition of "genuine." His conviction was that each

Christian had the obligation to exercise moral and spiritual discrimination, avoiding conformity with the standards of the society and allowing the transforming power of Christ to have its effect. The premise was set forth in Rom. 12:2: "Do not be conformed to this world, but be transformed by the renewal of your mind, that you may prove what is the will of God, what is good and acceptable and perfect." To "prove" what is "good" in a given situation requires the application of individual and collective intelligence, which was one reason Paul so vehemently opposed the authoritarian impulses of the "superapostles" in II Corinthians. This insistence on the need of collective judgment is visible in I Cor. 6:1–11, where Paul urges the congregation to adjudicate disputes between members, which were being tried in civil courts. It is also visible in a passage in Paul's earliest letter—to the Thessalonians—where charismatics and disciplinarians are at odds. He admonishes each side to be attentive to the distinctive contributions of their opponents: "Do not quench the Spirit, do not despise prophesying, but test everything; hold fast what is good, abstain from every form of evil" (I Thess. 5:19–22). The test of authenticity is never final, and it is never the exclusive prerogative of a single group. In Paul's view, it is an ongoing and never-ending task that requires the best resources within each community.

One of the illusions that can be traced through the history of tolerance in Western culture is that a final and universally accepted definition of what is "genuine" can be developed. The hope of Erasmus, for example, was that distinctions between the *fundamenta,* the fundamental element of faith, and the *adiaphora,* a term derived from the Pauline letters and referring to inconsequential matters, could be used to settle the disputes between Protestants and Catholics.[9] While it was appropriate for Erasmus to call for a discussion about where such distinctions should be drawn, it was futile to think that a lasting agreement could be reached. A variety of factors led the Unitarians and the later

Enlightenment thinkers to draw the line toward the left and orthodox thinkers to draw it toward the right. It is the kind of question that requires ongoing discussion on many levels, and the quality of a culture can be measured to some degree by the seriousness with which such discussion is conducted. I applaud Lance Morrow's call for the recovery of civil virtues, in the article cited at the beginning of this chapter, but I am skeptical of his suggestion that it may occur automatically as a result of the "mood" of the society: "It is possible that the '80s are going to demand some virtues unknown in the '60s and '70s—self-control, self-discipline, stoicism, decorum, even inhibition and a little puritanism. It may be time for a touch of reticence. Coercion cannot produce such attitudes, but the mood of the time may."[10]

I find more plausible the demand of John Gardner for public acknowledgment of the need for moral discrimination in the arts and criticism: "To avoid such judgments is to treat art as a plaything. . . . It is civilization's single most significant device for learning what must be affirmed and what must be denied."[11] In particular he calls upon artists to exercise discrimination as they assess each other's work: "Let artists say what they know, then, admitting the difficulties but speaking nonetheless. Let them scorn the idea of dismissing as harmless the irrelevant fatheads who steal museums and concert halls and library shelves: the whiners, the purveyors of high-tone soap opera, the calm accepters of senselessness, the murderers. . . . Let a state of total war be declared . . . between the age-old enemies, real and fake."[12] The imperative is not to achieve final definitions whether in art, politics, or ecclesiastical affairs, but to take part responsibly in the quest for what is genuine. A kind of intellectual and moral courage to decide in the midst of partial darkness, the distinctive product of holding the first two commandments in constant tension, is required to sustain this quest. What Paul calls for in the admonition, "Let love be genuine," is not that one can achieve final, authoritative solutions but that one should unceasingly address the task. I think his call is consistent with the final line of Glenn Tinder's statement that in the trying decades ahead, "we could lose our freedom not only by becoming hysterically and foolishly intolerant ... but also by not having the wit to limit tolerance when necessary in order to preserve its social and spiritual grounds."[13]

II

To "abhor" evil is the first of the qualifying statements that Paul uses to depict what it means to seek genuine love. The rare verb that Paul selects is surprisingly passionate and emotive. Its meaning in classical Greek is "hate violently, abhor,"[14] so that Sanday and Headlam appropriately observe, "The word expresses a strong feeling of horror."[15] To react to evil in this manner is usually thought to be more typical of zeal than love; one naturally associates the emotion of abhorrence with hatred, wrath, or envy. It seems a continent removed from tolerance, particularly as popularly understood—a pallid and weak acquiescence in whatever mischief others may devise. How can the authenticity of a tolerant love be measured by a criterion so highly charged and negative as this?

To pose the question in this manner reveals the extent to which liberal ideas about love and tolerance have come to dominate our appraisal of ancient texts. For Paul, it is obvious that if love does not lead one passionately to abhor that which thwarts love, it cannot by that measure be genuine. The depth of commitment to the value or person loved can be measured by the sense of horror at seeing them destroyed. Paul's choice of terms recalls the passion of parents protecting the life and health of their children, or that of a lover shielding his or her beloved. This is why there is more than mere humor in one of Prof. Laurence J. Peter's quotations: "I hate people who are intolerant."[16] It sounds at first like a funny contradiction, and might remain

at that level without the persistent reminder about "abhorring evil." If intolerance is not despised, that is a sure sign
that tolerance itself no longer commands sufficient emotional force to sustain itself.

The moral principle lying behind Paul's choice of the
term "abhorring" was set forth by Walter Berns in a recent
essay: "Anger is expressed or manifested on those occasions when someone has acted in a manner that is thought
to be unjust, and one of its origins is the opinion that men
are responsible, and should be held responsible, for what
they do. . . . Anger is somehow connected with justice. . . .
If, then, men are not angry when someone else is robbed,
raped, or murdered, the implication is that no moral community exists, because those men do not care for anyone
other than themselves. Anger is an expression of that
caring, and society needs men who care for one another,
who share their pleasures and their pains, and do so for the
sake of the others. It is the passion that can cause us to act
for reasons having nothing to do with selfish or mean
calculation. . . . A moral community is not possible without
anger and the moral indignation that accompanies it."[17] I do
not believe that one needs to follow the rest of Berns's
argument leading to support of capital punishment in order
to grasp what is at stake here. The capacity for abhorrence is
an index of the level of commitment to the truth and to the
well-being of others. It is therefore important for any theory
of tolerance to deal with the question of which evils are not
to be tolerated.

Glenn Tinder begins his discussion of this issue by
arguing: "The principle that we are justified in being
intolerant of all that destroys tolerance, and of all that
destroys the conditions rendering tolerance productive of
community and truth, seems to me unassailable in theory."
But he insists that such limits to tolerance "must be purely
circumstantial." While murder, robbery, and vandalism
destroy the order on which tolerance rests, it may also be
appropriate at times "to outlaw words leading to violence"

or to bar the "glamorization of violence" in popular entertainments. He tends to favor censorship of obscenities
which, "in depersonalizing, eradicate the mutual respect
on which a communal tolerance must depend." He is
particularly exercised by "one of the most serious problems
in America, the frivolity and baseness of most television
programs." In the era in which liberal theories of tolerance
were developed, he argues, a threat on this scale was not
envisioned, "but now, with the television networks monop-
olized by commerce and industry, it becomes apparent that
tolerance is mere weakness and folly if it cannot take
intelligent care of the conditions on which its value, and
even its continuance, depends."[18] Having written several
studies of the antidemocratic implications and effects of
some forms of mass entertainment,[19] I agree with Tinder's
assessment of the problem. When producers, sponsors, and
networks refuse to face such questions on the grounds that
it might infringe artistic freedom, they simply invite the
kind of vigilante activities that citizens committees are
exercising around the United States. The worst mistake of
all is to assume, as Norman Lear and his "freedom for the
media" movement do, that raising the question of limits is
somehow a violation of the principle of tolerance itself.

It is at this point that the principle of "counter-intolerance" suggested by Gabriel Marcel is so difficult to put into
practice.[20] Marcel distinguished between the "act of toler-
ating" and "tolerance" proper, which is a matter of responsiveness to the passionate commitments of others. When
one is aware of the depth as well as the fragility of one's
own deepest commitments, one thereby gains an empathy
for the differing commitments of others. To protect their
integrity as well as one's own requires tolerance in the form
of "the negation of a negation, a counter-intolerance"
directed against anything that would fail to guarantee such
commitments.[21] But how should I respond to those who
strive to set limits to my behavior at the very point where
my most passionate commitment to freedom of expression

is located? This is the issue currently separating the critics from the defenders of television entertainment. What if someone else's campaign to set appropriate limits to tolerance clashes with my commitment to "counter-intolerance"? It is wise in such circumstances to refrain from derogating one's opponents as irresponsible and intolerant, and to set about patiently arguing the merits of the case with all voices being heard. If it is intrinsic to tolerance to "abhor" evil, then several sides of the current debate over morality in the media have a legitimate role to play as far as the Pauline perspective is concerned. The present conflict is similar to that of the weak and the strong in Rome, whose tendency was to denounce each other, but whose obligation was to "welcome one another." Out of such public debate there may arise guidelines and insights that could go some distance toward ameliorating what is admittedly a very unhealthy situation—both in the mass media and in the style of the debate about the media. Tentative answers are the best that can be achieved, and even they are unlikely to be found if the passion of abhorring evil is repressed or discredited.

III

The final phrase of Paul's admonition in Rom. 12:9 is formulated in an equally passionate manner. Paul selects a verb[22] he has used elsewhere in his letters only to refer to marital intercourse, directly or by analogy (I Cor. 6:16–17; Eph. 5:31; cf. Matt. 19:5). Here Paul advises "cleaving to what is good." This is usually toned down by translators and commentators to something like "holding fast to what is good" (RSV). This is perhaps more seemly, but it has the disadvantage of eliminating a provocative range of semantic associations. Perhaps as a consequence of this translation tradition, none of the commentaries I have consulted point out the connections between the term translated "cleave to" and the broad tradition of Eros in Greek thought. The term *erōs* means love or sexual desire, and Eros of course is the god of love. Socrates taught that Eros was the desire for something good that one lacks. In the words of Werner Jaeger: "The concept of Eros becomes an epitome of all human striving to attain the good, . . . the desire 'to possess the good for ever.' . . . Eros for Socrates means the aspiration of the man who knows he is still imperfect, to mould his own spirit and his own reason, with his gaze steadily fixed on the Idea. It is in fact what Plato means by 'philosophy': the yearning of the true self within us to take shape."[23] The fact that the term *erōs* is avoided by New Testament writers has led scholars to dwell on the superiority of *agapē*, or disinterested love, over *erōs* as sensual love. This distinction tends to blind interpreters, however, to the occasional effort of a New Testament writer to evoke and adapt this rich philosophic tradition. Romans 12:9 is a case in point, for in selecting the associated term *kollaō*, "cleave to," Paul is able to avoid some of the pitfalls of the Socratic and Platonic views.

The Platonic tradition had assumed that *erōs* is always the desire for the good, the true, and the beautiful, and that people cannot desire what they think is bad for them. Paul's view is considerably more subtle, because he has faced the immutable reality that humans in fact choose the evil while seeking what they think is good or popular. The opening chapters of Romans lay out the evidence for this universal human reality, showing that all humans sin and fall short of what is truly good. Furthermore, the Platonic tradition had tended to pit the higher desires of the mind against the lower desires of the body, suggesting an educational strategy of mind over emotion that resulted in a dualistic anthropology. Paul recovers a unified anthropology that refuses to pit mind against body, arguing again in the early chapters of Romans that the refusal of the whole person to acknowledge the transcendent truth about God results in the distortion of both mind and body. When a person is restored to wholeness by faith in the gospel concerning the depth of human sin and the depth of divine love as revealed in the death and resurrection of Christ, the Platonic premise is in a sense restored. Those who have the "mind of Christ" are directed to think about "whatever is true, whatever is honorable, whatever is just, whatever is pure, whatever is lovely, whatever is gracious, ... any excellence, ... anything worthy of praise" (Phil. 4:8). In the wording of Romans, there is a need for the faithful to accept an ongoing transformation of "mind" in which the individual insight of faith is used to "prove what is the will of God, what is good and acceptable and perfect" (Rom. 12:2). It is not an automatic process, the inexorable result of *erōs*, but rather the act of a mind and will transformed and set free by divine *agapē*.

The verb translated "cleave to" in Rom. 12:9 is therefore much more suitable than *eraō*, the verbal form of *erōs*, for Paul's purpose. While evoking the semantic range of the Greek legacy of passionate attachment to the good, it depicts that attachment in terms of marital cleaving—the passionate, intentional covenanting of one's entire being to another. The direct parallels in I Corinthians reveal the kind of totally engrossing commitment that Paul has in mind: "Do you not know that he who cleaves to a prostitute becomes one body with her? ... But he who cleaves to the Lord becomes one spirit with him" (I Cor. 6:16–17). In Paul's view, the attraction leading to such cleaving is both powerful and intentional; it is so totally engrossing that a consideration of the consequences is required, which was Paul's concern in the debate over the legitimacy of prostitution in Corinth. In the case of marriage, Paul viewed such attraction as a charismatic gift (I Cor. 7:7) that needs to be honored and protected by covenantal bonds. Despite all barriers and risks, one enters into marital union in response to the power of this attraction, receiving the blessing of holiness when the covenant is maintained (I Thess. 4:1–7; I Cor. 7:14–16). To "cleave to the good" is to act in response to its powerful attraction, to be wedded to it with passionate intensity, despite all hindrances and ambiguities. Since this admonition comes to those who know from personal experience the perversities of both love and goodness, it requires a kind of postcritical "falling back in love" with the good and the true and the beautiful.

It is the context of the larger argument in Romans that preserves cleaving to the good from the danger of absolutism. Just as in marriage, where idolizing the partner is a sign of excessive dependency, immaturity, and weakness, so in the Pauline ethic there is no necessary connection between cleaving to the good and claiming that one's version of the good is in some sense final. Preserving the ongoing tension between the First and the Second Commandment and observing the specific warnings of Rom. 12:3 concerning "the measuring rod of faith" and the dangers of "super-mindedness" are required to keep this kind of postcritical passion within bounds. But these protective hedges should not be enlarged to the point that one's attraction to and commitment to the good are discredited.

Achieving an appropriate balance in the marriage to the good is difficult in any circumstances, but seems particularly so for a post-Puritan culture like our own. The long tradition of reforming, purifying, and liberating in American culture produces a mentality that delights in smashing idols. Although the religious rationale has dimmed, the cultural preference remains. We learn to take pleasure in destroying ideals, institutions, traditions, and leaders that fall short of the highest ideals. The consequence is that North Americans are always more comfortable saying what we are against than what we are for. It is easier for us to "abhor what is evil" than to "cleave to what is good." Earlier generations found it easier to accept traditional standards that defined the good. One thinks of the wide popularity of Alexander Pope's elegant lines in "An Essay on Criticism":

> First follow Nature, and your judgment
>   frame
> By her just standard, which is still the
>   same;
> Unerring Nature, still divinely bright,
> One clear, unchanged, and universal light,
> Life, force, and beauty must to all impart,
> At once the source, and end, and test of
>   Art.[24]

It is hard to imagine that current poets or readers, given our iconoclastic temperament, would create or enjoy the undaunted passion of John Keats's lines from "Endymion":

> A thing of beauty is a joy forever:
> Its loveliness increases; it will never
> Pass into nothingness; but still will keep
> A bower quiet for us, and a sleep
> Full of sweet dreams, and health, and quiet
>   breathing.[25]

The balance between skepticism about the content of human dogmas and the affirmation of ultimate truth that produced such resolute confidence in the poet Tennyson seems to go against the grain of our era:

> Our little systems have their day;
>   They have their day and cease to be;
>   They are but broken lights of thee,
> And thou, O Lord, art more than they.
>
> We have but faith: we cannot know,
>   For knowledge is of things we see;
>   And yet we trust it comes from thee,
> A beam in darkness: let it grow. . . .
>
> O, yet we trust that somehow good
>   Will be the final goal of ill,
>   To pangs of nature, sins of will,
> Defects of doubt, and taints of blood;
>
> That nothing walks with aimless feet;
>   That not one life shall be destroyed;

> Or cast as rubbish to the void,
> When God hath made the pile complete.[26]

Compared with these earlier affirmations of the good, the true, and the beautiful, current voices sound awkward even while enjoying the momentum of going against the stream of popular nihilism. The sure and elegant voice in John Gardner's novels and short stories gives way to strident declaration in *On Moral Fiction,* which seeks to make the point I am driving at here:

> True criticism, what I am calling "moral criticism," may speak of technique and sometimes ought to, but its ultimate concern is with ends.... The Good, the True, and the Beautiful are not, as everyone knows, things that exist in the way Llamas do, but values which exist when embodied and, furthermore, recognized as embodied.... They are values by definition, and by inspection not relative values but relative absolute values, like health.... It is precisely because art affirms values that it is important. The trouble with our present criticism is that criticism is, for the most part, not important. It treats the only true magic in the world as though it were done with wires.[27]

The difficulty in providing an adequate formulation and defense of the good was extensively documented in a two-part article by Bryan F. Griffin entitled "Panic Among the Philistines." He effectively pans the current literary establishment with glee. "The awful pallbearers of the century's shabby legacy—the leering old critics and the ghastly old novelists and the obsequious executive editors and the finger-snapping academics and the sleazy book clubs and the computerized publishers—had guided their cadaverous vessel over their private 'ocean of baseness' for so many tedious years that they could no longer remember where they had come from, or even why they had set out on the torturous voyage in the first place."[28] The essence of the "Philistine view of both art and life" is seeing "no link between the quality of the art and the quality of the life," in Griffin's view. He then goes on to speak of this as if it were some kind of geopolitical arrangement: "And that is what we are talking about, really: linkage, or the absence of linkage. Which is of course what Thoreau was talking about when he said that there was 'never an instant's truce between virtue and vice.' ... Art requires stricter judgments than life, because art must be more lucid in its virtue than life, or it is not art but decoration."[29] Though one may smile at the choice of terms, efforts such as Gardner's and Griffin's should be applauded. As is suggested by Paul's use of the word "cleave to," it is singularly difficult to explain or defend one's selection of a marital partner. At best it is a falling in love, a succumbing to the powerful attraction of the good, the true, and the beautiful. It may be appropriate for us in the final analysis, therefore, to be content with elusive reasons and simply to heed the admonition—to pull against the undertow of our era, to "cleave to what is good."

IV

The complex question of where the limits of tolerance should be drawn in a particular circumstance requires ongoing discussion, and Paul does not presume to provide final answers for the Romans. In the paragraphs that follow the key verse concerning the genuineness of love, however, Paul sets forth general ethical principles that offer guidelines for making such decisions. Tracing these guidelines seems particularly appropriate in a time such as ours when the moral landscape, so to speak, needs to be rediscovered.

In Rom. 12:10–16, there is a focus on the relations that love seeks to preserve within the community of faith. My translation of v. 10 brings the congregational setting within view:

> [having] affection for one another with
>   brotherly love,
> taking the lead in honoring one another
>   (Rom. 12:10)

The term "affection," which is ordinarily used for the close relations between friends and relatives, is used here for the first and only time in the New Testament. The closeness that would usually be expected in the spheres of intimacy implied by *philadelphia*, "brotherly love," is here extended into the realm of the church, which had become the arena of vicious conflict. The reciprocal scope of this "affection" is inclusive: it is affection "for one another." There is a translation problem in the second half of the verse, and the usual English verbs "esteeming" or "preferring" cannot be supported lexicographically. The basic meaning of the verb is "taking the lead," which corresponds to a Hebraic expression concerning the virtue of greeting strangers, visitors, and fellow synagogue members with generosity.[30] This simple and obvious translation has not been selected—in my opinion—because commentators and translators have not understood the relation of these verses to the congregational tensions in the Roman churches. In view of the background laid out in Chapter I, the verse suggests the guideline of generous welcome to competitors and ideological opponents within the congregation. It clearly gives priority to personal relations over ideological conformity, countering the tendency toward separating people into stereotypical groups, each convinced that the other is "evil."

The next verse counters the tendency of such an inclusive ethic to erode the enthusiasm that each side has for its particular ideological views and liturgical preferences, thus dividing the congregation:

> not flagging in eagerness,
>   remaining ebullient in spirit,
>   serving the Lord
>   (Rom. 12:11)

If one were to follow the ethic of the preceding verse and to honor one's ideological enemies, this might have a dampening effect on the "eagerness" and spiritual enthusiasm with which one maintains one's own position. The authentic origin of enthusiasm is depicted by the middle line: the apportioned spirit given to each Christian is to be allowed full reign, boiling up to produce the kind of enthusiasm that is capable of transcending differences in ideology. The final line about "serving the Lord" contains what Ernst Käsemann has discerned as a distinctive Pauline emphasis: The gift of the spirit is inseparable from its giver, the Lord, who extends his reign in and through the ecstatic experiences of Christians, which otherwise might become self-serving and prideful.[31] This verse seeks to retain the health of the life-giving stream of emotional fervor that produces and sustains tolerant love.

The next two verses evoke the dilemma of Christian love that so frequently is repudiated by a fallen world whose hostility extends into the relations between Christians themselves:

> rejoicing in hope,
>   persevering in persecution,
>   persisting in prayer,
> sharing in the needs of the saints,
>   pursuing love for strangers.
>   (Rom. 12:12–13)

To take one's joy "in hope" is not a matter of exulting in future triumphs that will overturn present dilemmas but rather, as shown by the paradoxical argument of Rom. 5:1–5, resting in the "peace with God" that holds firm through all adversities. Christian hope is an eschatological gift produced by the Spirit, by which "hope does not disappoint us, because God's love has been poured into our hearts through the Holy Spirit which has been given to us" (Rom. 5:5). What gives one the power to "persevere" in the face of "persecution" and lesser forms of antagonism is the vital *relationship* with God, which is why the succeeding line refers to prayer. The emphasis on "persisting" indicates that it is the ongoing relationship *between* the believer and

God that counts, rather than some quick and magical release from the burden of persecution. The final two lines draw attention back to the difficulties within the congregation in Rome, as I see it, because "sharing in the needs of the saints" implies taking up the burdens of those deported under Claudius who are returning to Rome at the time Paul writes. The term for the Jewish Christians, who as we know were the ones earlier banned from Rome, was typically "saints,"[32] and Paul's selection of a form of *koinōnia*, "sharing," conveys the broad sense of not only providing financial assistance but also shouldering the traumas of emotional adjustment. To "pursue" stranger-love, as the final line admonishes, is to revitalize the ethic of hospitality present in one form or another in both Greco-Roman and Hebraic cultures, actively reaching out to vulnerable travelers and émigrés to make them full members of one's community.

The next two verses (Rom. 12:14–15) continue the general ethical guidelines but do so with stylistic variations that reveal the citation of traditional material.[33] When one compares the wording "bless the persecutors" (found in many manuscripts) with the tradition in Matt. 5:44 and Luke 6:28 ("bless those who persecute you"), it is obvious that the omission of the second-person pronoun serves to broaden the admonition. In the Roman church situation, the traditional formulation would admonish only those who had actually experienced the persecution under Claudius, whereas Paul's formulation would also include those who had remained in Rome. To "bless and not curse" the persecutors does not imply, however, that anyone in the Roman church should condone the deportation. It commends an approach to moral ambiguity that persists in concern for one's adversaries, constantly requesting divine blessing rather than giving way to the utterance of damnations. The following admonitions to "rejoice with those who rejoice" and "weep with those who weep" continues this theme of personal concern and empathy. In a manner that transcends disagreements on policy and ideology, the members of the faithful community are to share and support one another's responses to evil and good. It is noteworthy that neither of these verses is limited to the community: the concern for the emotional and physical well-being of others extends in principle to everyone.

A very literal translation of Rom. 12:16 reveals the bearing of guidelines on the highly charged religious and intellectual differences that were holding the Roman Christians back from unity:

> Be of the same mind toward one another. Do not set your minds on exalted things, but be drawn to lowly persons. Never be [wise-] minded in yourselves. (Rom. 12:16)

The connection between "wise-minded" and the favored mottoes of early Christian radicals as "the wise-minded ones" (I Cor. 4:10; 10:15; II Cor. 11:19) has led scholars to believe that Paul derived these admonitions from his experience with ecstatics and Gnostics.[34] There were some first-century intellectuals of Gnostic background who claimed a self-sufficient wisdom tantamount to divinity. In such instances conceit was raised to a philosophical principle, based on the notion of a spark of the divine glowing in every Gnostic. The potential of such sentiments to destroy community is countered by the central admonition in Rom. 12:16 concerning the alternative of directing oneself either toward "exalted things" or toward "lowly persons." Rather than allowing one's intellectual powers to abstract one from concrete personal circumstances, the person pursuing genuine love will enter into sympathetic relations with the less enlightened. In this sense I believe that the expression "being of the same mine toward one another" means acknowledging mental equality. Rather than giving way to a culturally defined premise of the superiority of intellectuals, Paul insists on an admission that in comparison with divine wisdom, human differences are insignificant. Godet captures this aspect of Paul's intention more adequately than any current commentator: "The antipathy felt by the apostle to every sort of spiritual aristocracy, to every caste distinction within the church" reaches a crescendo at the end of this verse.[35] From the perspective of our question concerning the limits of tolerance, the principle of equality constitutes a permanent guideline in the inevitable conflicts between differing standards.

A crucial issue in setting limits for tolerance is dealt with in Rom. 12:17–20, overcoming the rule of retaliation against evildoers. Paul begins with what appears to be a traditional theme of early Christian catechism, "Never repay evil for evil."[36] When confronted by the typical behavior of a fallen world, aggression, disrespect, and exploitation, the Christian is to refuse to respond in kind. The cycle of violence must be broken somewhere and replaced by "good." It is interesting at this point that Paul evokes the public standard of "taking thought for what is good in relation to all persons" (v. 17). Consultation with the secular community as well as the community of faith is demanded by this inclusive expression. The data that should inform Christian ethics include discovering the motivations of one's adversaries as well as the social conditions from which their hostile actions arise. The goal toward which one should strive in such "good" response and decisions is set forth in realistic terms:

> If possible, so far as it depends on you, be at peace with all persons. (Rom. 12:18)

The qualifications at the beginning of this admonition reveal that Paul was not a pacifist. In his view there are times when peace is not possible, when circumstances call for forcible reactions to evil. Paul's concern is that one should strive for the goal of peace and that no excuses should be accepted that confuse one's own hostility with the behavior of one's adversaries. There is no basis here for mounting preemptive attacks in order to eliminate the possibility of aggressive action by potential enemies, the rationale that so frequently masks the aggressive quality and intention of one's own responses to evil. Given the emotional confusion doubtless caused by threats of aggression against the life and property of a Christian in that day, there was a need for the kind of counterbalance of public wisdom that is suggested in the preceding verse, to guide one's response.

The principle of never being a judge in one's own interest or cause, embodied in Greco-Roman and Jewish as well as modern jurisprudence, is at stake in the next admonition:

> Beloved, do not avenge yourselves, but give place to wrath. For it is written, "Vengeance is mine, I will repay," says the Lord. (Rom. 12:19)

In the face of the popularity of vengeance in the entertainments, politics, and foreign policy of Rome, Paul insists on leaving the ultimate balancing of justice to God. This does not erode the necessity of public institutions of justice, as the early verses of Romans 13 make plain. Nor does it question the ultimate need for vengeance, a balancing out of the disparities between crime and punishment in a vicious world. Definitely excluded is taking the law into one's own hands, the kind of personal vengeance that every civilized system of impartial justice seeks to prevent. In particular, given the zealous sentiments of a large portion of the Jewish community in the period prior to the Jewish-Roman war of A.D. 66–70, Paul excludes vigilante actions by self-appointed Jehu figures. Zealotism is presumptuous, Paul insists, for it refuses to "give way" to the prerogatives of divine justice. God alone is capable of proper vengeance. This verse has a particular bearing on modern embodiments of zealous vigilantism in which millions of citizens prepare themselves with weapons and paramilitary training to protect and avenge themselves, guided by the heroic myths of popular entertainments that such violence creates true justice.

Paul's alternative to zealous vigilantism is not passivity but instead an active concern for the life and well-being of one's adversary:

> Instead, if your enemy is hungry, feed him; if he is thirsty, give him drink. For in so doing you heap coals of fire on his head. (Rom. 12:20)

This verse specifies by example what was meant earlier by not repaying evil for evil. The natural tendency is to respond to violence with violence or to counter meanness with reprisals, and actions of mercy aim to break the deadly cycle. The abiding guideline of a tolerant community is the commitment to "overcome evil with good," as set forth in the climactic summary of the succeeding verse. William Klassen has made a convincing case that the metaphor of burning charcoal on the head depicts repentance and remorse on the part of the adversaries rather than painful vengeance enacted against them.[37] Paul's strategy seeks not only the well-being but also the transformation of persecutors. There is of course no assurance that the specific response one selects in a conflict situation will actually produce this result. Those who speak of Paul as an incurable optimist at this point[38] confuse intentions with results. As Paul knew from personal experience, there are some adversaries who react to being shamed by such unanticipated gestures of love by redoubling the intensity of their hatred. No facile promises are implied in 12:20. Paul simply directs attention at the end of his discussion to the distinction between good and evil and the task of seeking the transformation of the latter by the former. Rather than allowing victimage to triumph by submitting to its terms and means, the Christian is to participate in the restoration of the goodness of the created order: "Do not be overcome by evil, but overcome evil with good" (Rom. 12:21).

The context of repudiating zealous rebellion is crucial for the interpretation of Paul's guidelines for setting limits in relation to the government. Romans 13:1–7, one of the best known, if not to say notorious, paragraphs in the Pauline corpus, has frequently been understood as demanding total subservience to whatever the government demands. Particularly in the traditional Lutheran or Anglican exegesis, Rom. 13:1 ("Let every person be subject to the governing authorities. For no authority exists except by God's appointment, and the authorities in power have been ordained by God") has been taken as requiring unquestioning obedience to rulers from George III and Frederick the Great to Adolf Hitler.[39] Several recent studies have thrown light on the historical circumstances addressed by the seemingly general admonitions in this passage, revealing that Paul was not necessarily intending to create a permanently binding ethic of submission. Marcus Borg has made a case for the presence of "anti-Roman sentiments" on the part of the Jewish community in Rome, leading it to sympathize with the zealot resistance movement that was carrying out the guerrilla warfare in Israel at the time of the writing of Romans. The basic point of Rom. 13:1–7 is thus stated by Borg: "Your obligation to Israel cannot encompass participation in their cause against Rome. . . . Christ bridges the chasm—but Jewish nationalism can only widen it, first, because it perpetuates the incorrect theological notion that God's purpose is primarily for the Jews, and second, because of the social and military hostility which it engenders between Jew and Gentile."[40]

In particular, Borg argues that when Paul states that the civil authority "does not bear the sword in vain" (Rom. 13:4), it is the "warmaking ability of the Roman state" rather than the power of judicial punishment that is in view.[41] Although I am inclined to think that the judicial use of capital punishment cannot be eliminated, the issue of rebellion was nevertheless in view. This connects directly with the theme of "vengeance" in 12:19–21 when one takes the zealot rationale for the Jewish-Roman war into account. Finally, Borg suggests that the idea of the government being "God's servant for your good" (Rom. 13:4) had a specifically Christian connotation that bears rather directly on the theme of tolerance: "Since salvation for Paul is fundamentally corporate and involves the reconciliation of Jew and Gentile into one body, the Roman government contributes to this work of Christ ('your good') to the extent that it restrains the perpetuation of that particularity which partially produced the hostility. Thus Paul's advice to the Roman Christians to subject themselves to Rome was [given] . . . also because participation in Israel's cause would defeat a central purpose of the gospel for which Christ died."[42]

Several years after Borg's article appeared, a team of German scholars addressed the issues in Rom. 13:1–7 from the perspective of the controversy over excessive taxes that erupted in the Nero administration several years after the writing of Romans. They pointed out that the positive reference to taxation in vs. 6–7 is unparalleled in Jewish literature of the Greco-Roman period and is therefore likely to be emphatic. Paul's terms for "taxes" and "customs duties" that ought to be paid are the precise Greek translations of the Latin terms concerning the disputed revenues referred to by Suetonius.[43] The intent of Paul's ethical guidelines was to warn against political agitation in the period when public resistance to taxation was intensified and when the Roman authorities had recently relaxed the edict banning Jewish and Christian agitators from the city. "The guidelines of Paul in Rom. 13:1–7, which appear to us today so basic and abstract, therefore, had for the Christians in Rome in the period around A.D. 56 a highly current and concrete meaning. The situation of those who ought to attempt to overcome the evils confronting them by doing good deeds was very real for them, and at the same time the occasion for Paul to advise the Roman congregations in their current political circumstances."[44]

Two additional aspects must be taken into account in evaluating Paul's advice about the authorities. He writes in the period prior to the first imperial persecution of Christians under Nero that evolved out of the burning of Rome in the summer of A.D. 64. In fact, at the time Paul wrote Romans, the Nero administration, in the hands of Seneca and Burrus, was being conducted with exemplary judicial fairness and honesty. It was not until six years later, in the spring of A.D. 62, that Nero's regime began to turn in a paranoid direction, resulting in summary execution of political opposition both real and imagined.[45] Compared with the lawless harassment that Paul had known at the hands of Jewish zealots, Roman administration in the mid-50s appeared reasonable and supportive of the conditions necessary for the conduct of the Christian mission. This assessment can be related to the evidence set forth by August Strobel and W. C. van Unnik that the administrative terminology in Rom. 13:1–7 was in use by the bureaucrats in the imperial regime who correlated Hellenistic and Roman terms in their bilingual administration of the empire.[46] Since at least two of the five house churches in Rome were located in such administrative circles (Rom. 16:10–11), Paul's positive appraisal of the legitimacy of their efforts to maintain law and order and his accurate use of their bureaucratic languages served the ambassadorial purposes of Romans. Paul certainly could not hope to gain the support of such circles in the difficult mission west to Spain by lending his prestige to the tax resistance and zealous rebellions that were brewing. The circumstances of his missionary experience and requirements were congruent with the relative fairness of the imperial administration at the moment, allowing him to develop a thoroughly positive rationale for compliance with regulations.

In view of the specific circumstances in Rome at the time of writing Rom. 13:1–7, it is noteworthy that Paul carries out the ethic of freely responsible love while insisting throughout on the criterion of "genuine." This is visible in the elimination of subservience and fear in the motivation of the ethic. While the authorities are a threat to evildoers, they approve of those who do good (13:3), so there is no reason for terror. What is required is "willing subordination" to regulations (13:1), "not only to avoid God's wrath but also for the sake of conscience" (13:5). Since Christians know of the divinely ordained purpose of government, they would suffer conscience pangs if they refused to submit to its requirements.[47] The commitment to distinguishing between good and evil that connects the ethic in this paragraph with the thesis statement of 12:9 would be violated if Christians complied simply out of fear of reprisals. This appears to correlate with the symmetry between obligations and performance that climaxes the paragraph. One is not to treat the authorities with the kind of servility that implies they are more divine than human. The theme of limited obligations, freely fulfilled, is eloquently stated:

> Pay them all what is owed: taxes to whom taxes are due; customs duties to whom customs duties are due, respect to whom respect is due, honor to whom honor is due. (Rom. 13:7)

This theme is picked up in the final section of the ethical guidelines: "Owe no one anything except this: To love one another." The entire obligation of the religious and moral law of the Old Testament is integrated into this system, in that all of the Ten Commandments are "summed up in the saying, 'You shall love your neighbor as yourself'" (Rom. 13:9). The final point that "love is the fulfilling of the law" (13:10) eliminates the final shred of rationale for the Christian antinomianism that posed a threat to the Roman congregations and lurks as a constant danger to any ethic of love. The ongoing usefulness of the law as a guideline for Christian ethics is here affirmed, while the motivation of genuine love is kept at the center of action. C. E. B. Cranfield provides a responsible summary:

> To draw the conclusion from Paul's statement that love is the fulfilling of the law that we can therefore afford to forget the Ten Commandments and all the rest of the Law ... would be altogether mistaken. For, while we most certainly need

the summary to save us from missing the wood for the trees
and from understanding the particular commandments in a
rigid, literalistic, unimaginative, pedantic, or loveless way,
we are equally in need of the particular commandments, into
which the law breaks down the general obligation of love, to
save us from resting content with vague, and often hypocriti-
cal, sentiments.[48]

I would only add that the entire context of the Pauline ethic
from 12:1 through 13:14 should be kept in view when one
reads Cranfield's proviso, because Paul does not reinstate
an ethic of law. His starting point remains intact: Each
Christian has the obligation to "prove what is the will of
God, what is good and acceptable and perfect" (12:2). The
law simply remains a useful guideline for setting limits for
love and for enacting love responsibly in the complex
situations that one must assess on a daily basis. It would be
a serious misunderstanding of the tolerant ethic of Paul to
conclude that he condones finding easy answers about what
the limits of love should be simply by reinstating legalism.

The eschatological intensification that concludes the
general ethic of Romans 13 eliminates complacency of any
kind. Unfortunately, careless translation of the opening
words of 13:14 tends to destroy the connection that Paul
had in mind:[49]

> Moreover, you know what time it is. The hour already [calls]
> you to awake out of sleep. For our salvation is nearer now
> than when we first believed. The night is far spent, the day
> is at hand. Let us then cast off the works of darkness . . . Let
> us act as is fitting for the day . . . But put on the Lord Jesus
> Christ and do not make provisions for the flesh to satisfy its
> desires. (Rom. 13:11–14)

The intense expectation of the end of time is palpable in
this passage, but it does not lead to ethical or intellectual
relaxation. In fact, it is precisely because Paul was conscious of the inbreaking of the new age, and of its transformation of every form of legalistic and societal conformity,

that he insists so vigorously on the need to evaluate every guideline and act in a manner appropriate "for the day." The final words provide a clear reference back to "genuine love" in 12:9, revealing that Paul felt the need to counter libertinistic tendencies to "make provisions for the flesh" in the manner of the Corinthian Gnostics.[50] That one should find ways to "vent" the desires of the flesh, in order that they no longer disturb the equilibrium of the spirit, is explicitly repudiated. The limits of tolerance are finally grounded in the new age that Christ inaugurated. Against the pressures that the old age continues to exert both inside and outside the circle of believers, the task of "casting off the works of darkness" remains constant. To know "what time it is" is also to know that the present is a "far spent" night, so that yesterday's pronouncements and strategies are no longer necessarily apt. Setting limits for tolerant communities of faith is an ongoing challenge requiring the resources of the entire body of Christ, both past and present. To set limits and to proclaim the freedom to live creatively within them without ever claiming finality is what is required for those who have "put on the Lord Jesus Christ" in order to live in "the day" of his truth.

Chapter V

GUIDELINES
FOR
TOLERANT CONGREGATIONS

In his account of the tragic schism between conservative and moderate Lutherans that occurred in the Lutheran Church—Missouri Synod in 1974, Frederick W. Danker cites the prophetic warning that was issued almost thirty years earlier. Forty-two leaders of the denomination met in Chicago in 1945 to discuss the increasingly acrimonious atmosphere, issuing a statement deploring the "loveless attitude ... expressed in suspicions of brethren, in the impugning of motives, and in the condemnation of all who have expressed differing opinions concerning some of the problems confronting our Church today." One of the signers of this statement, Theodore Graebner of Concordia Seminary, uttered a warning that proved remarkably accurate: "Legalism and a loveless zeal for orthodoxy is going to breed radicalism, liberalism, strife and division."[1] By falling into such destructive patterns of interaction, the church was in effect committing itself to a course that would lead to eventual civil war.

Our reflections on the legacy of Paul in Romans have been guided from the start by the realization that he confronted a situation somewhat analogous to our own: a social setting in a world marked by relativism and degeneracy, a religious situation in which extreme options were offered, ranging from zealous battle against the social order on the one hand to ascetic withdrawal on the other, and a church situation in Rome marked by hostile conflict between liberals and conservatives in which racial, temperamental, and ideological factors contributed to divisiveness. The guidelines he developed in that situation seem to have peculiar relevance in our era, when the entire culture is drifting toward hostile conflict. How did Paul propose to cope with the competition between liberals and conservatives, Greeks and Romans and Jews, in order to achieve the ideal of tolerance?

I

In order to gain perspective on the innovative guidelines Paul developed, I would like to provide the basis for some comparisons. There are at least five distinctive attitudes toward pluralism within Christian communities, and only one of them seems congruent with the view expressed in Romans. These can be briefly sketched as follows:

Avoid pluralism or doctrinal diversity of any kind in the Christian community. For example, some voices in the "church growth" movement advise recruiting only people from one's own class and from like-minded sorts of people. The preference, when establishing new congregations, is to found them in relatively uniform suburbs or sections of cities or towns to achieve unity, which involves having people from only one cultural level and only one ideological background. In the doctrinal area, this kind of viewpoint of avoiding pluralism at all costs has been advocated by theologians and church leaders such as Francis A. Schaeffer. His recent book, *The Church Before the Watching World,* calls for a strict separation between people who share his view of orthodoxy and those who do not. In his view the call of God is to "simultaneously practice the orthodoxy of doctrine and the orthodoxy of community in the visible church."[2] He makes it plain that fellowship within the church is to be maintained only with those who have his view of verbal inspiration, and that others who have alternative perspectives should be avoided, particularly within the church. They are to be ranked as part of the watching world and the demonic forces that have opposed the church from the beginning of time. Here is a typical summary of Schaeffer's view: "We who have bowed before God's verbalized, propositional communication—the Bible—and before the Christ of that Bible, are brothers in Christ. This we must do in the face of liberal theology. We must practice an observable and real oneness—before God, before the elect ancients, before the demonic hosts, before the watching liberals and before the watching world."[3] When a church falls below one's level of doctrinal purity, Schaeffer's advice is that one ought to leave: "If the battle for doctrinal purity is lost, we must understand that there is a second step to take in regard to the practice of purity in the visible church. It may be necessary for true Christians to leave this visible organization with which they have been associated."[4] Clearly, the strategy of Schaeffer and others like him is to avoid pluralism at any price.

Tone it down. This approach appears to sidestep the question of pluralism: to allow it to exist, but not to allow it to stand in the way of the growth of a particular congregation. In the portion of the "church growth" movement influenced by Robert H. Schuller, this perspective takes the form of advice that leaders interested in church growth should avoid conflicts and controversial issues. They should allow no divisive question to impede the growth of their congregation. "Controversy has been a major cause of membership decline in Protestantism," Schuller writes.[5] Where there are divisive controversies, they should be set aside or played down as much as possible. This takes the form of being very careful to allow no one with controversial views to hold a position of leadership, or at least, if such persons are allowed, to make certain that they never have enough votes to determine policy. Schuller reports that he changed the by-laws of the Garden Grove Community Church when "a negative-thinking minority in the church succeeded in manipulating appointments" to a key committee. Now, he writes, "I, as senior minister, . . . appoint the chairmen of all these committees to the church board for their approval. By appointing the committee chairmen, by being an ex officio member of each committee, by being the chief of the staff presiding over regular staff meetings, I am able to maintain leadership control over the entire operation of the church."[6] With this approach, whenever conflicts arise, or when the results of genuine pluralism manifest themselves, they should be toned down and the representatives of the various sides maintained within the church.

Melt it in. In this particular view there is an effort to incorporate minority groups into a single dominant group. One finds this same attitude in the melting-pot concept of unity within the United States of America. In the case of churches with high doctrinal standards this takes the form of requiring relatively extreme levels of adherence to doctrinal and behavioral patterns. If people come from other classes or social groups, they are urged to adopt dress patterns and life-style forms which the majority have already found appropriate. For example, in Jerry Falwell's church and college there are very strict guidelines both for belief and appearance. The Liberty Baptist College student handbook insists that men should wear ties and women dresses to all classes. "Hair should be cut in a way that it does not come over the ear or collar. Beards or mustaches are not permitted." For women, "dresses and skirts . . . shorter than two inches [below] the middle of the knee are unacceptable," and so forth.[7] Such guidelines produce a strict division between those belonging to Falwell's organization and all others. In this kind of approach to pluralism any genuine pluralistic option must be either absorbed or eliminated.

Fight it out. This is the perspective which seems to have been followed very widely in the church politics of the last forty or fifty years. Perhaps it has always been followed to some degree, but we are seeing a vigorous form of this perspective at the present time in the sentiments of the Moral Majority, who are exercising their formidable political power, not only within the secular order of politics and public affairs but also within denominations such as the Southern Baptist Convention, the Presbyterian churches, and the Lutheran Church—Missouri Synod. The motto of this group is "50 percent plus one." The means of democratic order are to be used and forcibly seized by people who have the right doctrinal approach, and they are to force others to conform to their views. But this perspective of eliminating pluralism by the democratic process has in effect ruled church people out of church leadership positions or out of the seminaries when they have ended up on the losing side of political battles. This strategy has resulted in major divisions in the Presbyterian churches as well as in the Lutheran Church—Missouri Synod in the past decade. It has seriously threatened the unity of the Southern Baptist Convention. And there are indications that a number of other American denominations have been threatened by this kind of strategy. As Martin E. Marty has remarked on several occasions: "All the real bloodletting in American church life these days is within denominations, rather than between them." Unlike the conflicts within the political realm, where losers still retain their rights, the losers in ecclesiastical battles very often are completely destroyed and forced to leave the denominations where they have worked all their lives. Romans seems quite relevant to this particular pattern, because it is reminiscent of the pattern that the Roman Christians themselves apparently had been following when Paul wrote to them.

Let it flourish. This is the perspective that Paul appears to be following in the epistle to the Romans, as we have seen on the basis of our earlier study. If Christians of both conservative and liberal perspectives are to "welcome one another" in the Roman congregation, this clearly means that the differences between groups are to be allowed to stand. Indeed, they are to be encouraged, because the integrity of each side is to be respected. Paul's attitude at this point is reminiscent of one of the classic proposals for social tolerance in Western culture. Jean Bodin, in his *Colloquium* (1593), takes up the ideal of respectful conversation without, so far as I can tell, being explicitly dependent on Romans. He depicts extensive dialogues between a Calvinist, a Lutheran, an Italian Catholic, a Jew, a follower of Islam, a rationalist, and a naturalist. They discuss their differences and then part, having agreed to disagree. They hear the words, "Lo, how good and pleasing it is for brothers to live in unity, arranged not in common diatonics or chromatics, but in enharmonics, with a certain or divine modulation." They take their pleasure in their diversity within unity, each embracing the other "in mutual love."[8] What Bodin was only able to imagine, Paul in Romans seeks to bring into reality, with a rationale that is considerably more profound. We turn now to the practical guidelines Paul devised to allow a Christian pluralism to flourish.

II

The argument that Paul develops in Romans 14 and 15 in favor of conducting the Christian congregation so as to sustain tolerant relationships begins with the idea of the servant-Lord relationship. On the basis of this, Paul argues for the elimination of strategies of conformity that were widely used in Rome at the time, just prior to the writing of this letter. We can see the distinctive form of these strategies of conformity, on the basis of Paul's wording of the argument in chs. 14 and 15. The first of these strategies is that which was apparently being followed by the conservatives in the Roman house churches. It can be summed up in the word "judging." We first find a reference to this in 14:3, when Paul writes, "Let not him who abstains pass judgment on him who eats; for God has welcomed him." The same motif is picked up in v. 10: "Why do you pass judgment on your brother?" and once again in v. 13: "Then let us no more pass judgment on one another." This particular strategy of conformity aims at the underachiever. It is what one might call the bad-grade syndrome. When one judges someone as falling below the standard expected for performance, there is the implicit threat of impending judgment. In the language of Transactional Analysis, one might say that this particular strategy tells people who do not conform to the moral standards of the conservatives in Rome: You are not O.K. Your problem is that you fall below the line. If one were to draw a cartoon version of this particular strategy of conformity, it would clearly be a frown. The effort is to make deviants who fall below the norm feel guilty about their performance and raise it up to conform to the pattern expected by the majority.

A somewhat different strategy of conformity was used by the liberals in Rome, and its mark was "despising." There is clearly a reference to this general pattern in 14:3: "Let not him who eats despise him who abstains." One finds the same motif in 14:10b: "Or you, why do you despise your brother?" This pattern of behavior, obviously followed by the so-called "strong" in Corinth, aimed at enforcing conformity with those perceived to be overachieving. This is the kind of method used against "A-plus" students. Others seek to undermine their morale by calling them "mama's boys" or "nice people" or "the straights." The strategy of despising aims at undermining the self-image of people who achieve too well. It seeks to reduce others to a lower level of performance. To use once again the terms of Transactional Analysis, this particular strategy says in effect, "You are not O.K., because you are too O.K.!" If one were to draw a cartoon version of this particular strategy of conformity, it would be the sneer.

The unspoken premise of both strategies is that the standard followed by those persons who judge and despise is normative for all others. The problem with this premise, of course, in Paul's view, is that it makes such persons in the Roman congregation into lords of each other. The whole purpose of those who demand conformity is to demonstrate that they are better than all the others and that they can rule them, because they know better than the others. Many elements contribute to this sense of superiority. There are racial, theological, temperamental, historical, and tradition-al reasons for people being threatened by one another or feeling that their norm is superior to the ones that others are following. The problem is basic to any community of faith, which tends to raise such preferences and traditions to the level of final legitimacy.

Recent studies in "faith development" by James W. Fowler and Jack Renard Pressau clarify the dynamics of competition and the demands of conformity that Paul was dealing with in Rome.[9] On the basis of the theories of Piaget, Erikson, and Kohlberg, they suggest six stages of faith that move from preconventional faith through conven-tional to postconventional outlooks. While these stages match the growth of cognitive and evaluative abilities to some degree, they can be correlated with belief systems and patterns of interaction. Although the research in this area is not sufficiently advanced to make cross-cultural comparisons fully plausible, it is possible to suggest that the "weak" in Rome were at preconventional and conven-tional levels of faith and morality. They felt bound by traditional patterns of worship and ethics derived in part from their previous conditioning. The "strong" in Rome sound very much like the higher level of conventionalists, involved in what Fowler has described as the demytholo-gizing process of "individuative-reflective faith," or the first stage of postconventionalism[10] which, according to Pressau, often involves elements of moral relativism.[11] They felt themselves released from the inferior norms of traditional ethics and theology and felt superior to the so-called "weak." The interaction between persons on differ-ent levels of faith development often involves the kind of friction Paul was countering in Rome, and Pressau suggests why. If a religious appeal uses language suitable for lower levels of development than a person is on, he observes, "the person may feel condescension toward it; while if it is two or more stages above that level, the person will not understand it and will probably find it threatening."[12] The strategies of "judging" and "despising" in Rome seem to match this description rather closely.

The argument that Paul develops to counter strategies of conformity is to clarify the element of presumption. The litmus test is whether an action disturbs the relation between the Lord and any of his householders. This is visible in the declaration that one finds at the end of Rom. 14:3. Both the "weak" person and the "strong" person are using the strategies of judging and despising the other, and each is told to desist, "for God has welcomed him." Although the singular term "him" is used in this verse, Käsemann has argued rightly that in principle it includes both sides.[13] This point was elaborated earlier in connection with 15:7 when the implications of mutual welcome were laid out. The basis of this theory of welcome is set forth in the entire argument of the epistle to the Romans. If God declares my opponent "O.K.," who am I to question it? This point is argued in the subsequent passage in Romans 14–15 by means of the earliest Christian confession. The "Lordship of Christ" category was basic in the creedal formation of early Christianity. To be in Christ was to be under the Lordship of the Resurrected One. The argument in Romans 6 is particularly in view at this point, namely, that those who are in Christ belong to the sphere of Christ and are under his Lordship and power alone, and that therefore they are not the slaves of any other creature or any other force on earth.

Paul's argument is driven home by the rhetorical question of Rom. 14:4: "Who are you to pass judgment on the householder of another? It is before his own master that he stands or falls, and he will be upheld, for the master is able to make him stand." My translation takes account of Paul's peculiar selection of the term *oiketēs,* "householder" ("member of the household") in place of "slave" or "servant." Paul's word is similar to that used in Gal. 6:10 ("the household of faith") and Eph. 2:19 ("the household of God"), in honorific descriptions of Christians as beloved members of the family. I believe that Paul selected this term in place of "slave" in this instance because he wished to stress, not the subordination of Christian disciples to their Lord, but rather the distinctive position of honor which they hold as members of the household. The "someone else" in this verse, who is the Lord of the household, is of course Christ himself, as the elaboration of this theme in Rom. 14:10–12 reveals. Each member of the Lord's household must face the final judgment alone. One's responsibility is direct and aimed toward God rather than primarily toward neighbor, so that no one will have to account for another's actions. Also no one will be able to excuse himself or herself because someone else has failed in a more flagrant manner. "So each of us will give account of himself" (Rom. 14:12). Paul too is included in the company of those who must give account.

The effect of this argument is severalfold. It shows up the strategies of conformity as presumptuous. The demand to conform loses sight of who is truly the Lord and what the Lord has already declared about the legitimacy of the other side: They were "accepted" by grace alone—regardless of their conformity to works, no matter how measured. Differences in maturity of faith development, to use the modern term, are radically altered and legitimated by this acceptance motif. In effect, both judging and despising are shown up in this argument as violations of the First and Second Commandments. Those who demand conformity fail to see who is really the Lord of the earth.

The other thrust of this argument is to reinforce equality. The assumption of any strategy of conformity is that I am in a sense better than you. I am exempt from criticism, while you are either below or above the appropriate level of performance. But with his argument Paul reasserts the theme of individual accountability, which was basic to early Christian ethics. Whether you conform to the law as a conservative or feel freed from the law as a liberal, you are not O.K. by virtue of that behavior. You remain accountable, and it is the transcendent Lord alone who will judge. He has a direct relationship with each person, no matter what the level of moral and cognitive development. Therefore, the judgment that we make upon ourselves, though necessary at times, is never to be viewed as absolute. Romans 14:11 reiterates the early Christian hymnic and confessional theme that "every knee shall bow and every tongue shall give praise" to God and not to human conformity or nonconformity. Whenever this argument is eroded, the essential basis for Christian equality collapses as well. But when this is maintained, any strategy of conformity is thereby set aside. The result of this argument is the robust autonomy of individual believers. If each person stands before the same Lord, with none having the right to interfere or criticize the other, a basic autonomy results. By that I mean each person has a need for integrity, and while codes may differ, no one has a formula that can rightfully be imposed on others. Some members of the Roman community of Christians are committed to a liturgical calendar, says Paul in Rom. 14:5ff., while others feel free from the obligation to observe holy days. Paul does not say they must all agree with one view or compromise so that each gets a portion of what he or she thinks is right, but says rather: "Let each one be fully convinced in his own mind" (Rom. 14:5). The astounding implications of this view are caught by Ernst Käsemann: "The principle does not render discussion of particular points useless, but decisively sanctions different perspectives on the concrete situation.... An unending breadth of possibilities opens up for the church as a whole as well as for the individual.... Where this is not possible, Christianity splits into sects."[14] Here is the theoretical basis for a genuine Christian pluralism.

The danger of such pluralism, of course, is that it becomes indistinguishable from license. This is why in various ways throughout Romans 14–15 Paul formulates the principle that "whatever does not proceed from faith is sin" (Rom. 14:23). In this verse Paul does not attempt to state a comprehensive doctrine of sin, as we have suggested earlier, but rather to summarize the point about personal autonomy. As long as one is true to the particular form of Christian behavior which one feels is legitimate and consistent with his or her own personal faith, says Paul, and acts in direct responsibility to God, it must be accepted as legitimate. To act according to an alien norm is not to act "from faith," but is to destroy the basic relationship with the Lord that the gospel has established. Thus Paul can argue: "He who observes the day, observes it in honor of the Lord. He also who eats, eats in honor of the Lord, since he gives thanks to God; while he who abstains, abstains in honor of the Lord and gives thanks to God" (Rom. 14:6). The passage is carefully balanced so that the legitimacy of the conservatives and the liberals alike is acknowledged, in equal measure. It is obviously the conservative who "observes the day" in the cultic calendar, and the liberal who "eats," but both do so in honor of the Lord and both give thanks. Even the one who refrains from eating, namely, in this case the conservative, does so with thanks. It may seem strange that a person would give thanks for what he or she does not eat, but the point that Paul has in mind here is to equalize the legitimacy of both sides.

What we have here in Romans is a charismatic, relational form of human autonomy. It is not absolute autonomy, as in secular liberalism. The autonomy of believers in Romans is charismatic in that it is based on the gift of faith, evoked by the Spirit in response to the gospel. The relational aspect is particularly stressed in Rom. 14:4, 7–9. These references to the "Master" or "Lord," before whom one stands or falls, and to "giving thanks to God" and "living to the Lord" make it clear that it is the one-to-one relationship between the believer and Christ which is in view. No one is to subvert this relationship which each person in faith has with the Lord, because it is "before his own Lord that he stands or falls. And he will be upheld, for the Lord is able to make him stand"—as Paul argues in v. 4. Paul insists that the autonomy of Christian believers is not absolute; it is based on the relationship that the Lord has inaugurated, a relationship that, like marriage in the Jewish and Christian traditions, admits no incursion by outsiders. Paul appears to be sensitive to the threat of other forms of autonomy in vs. 7–9. Gnosticism, for example, tended toward an absolute form of individual autonomy, because each person had a spark of the divine, and when it was discovered through "knowledge," the person in a sense became divine. One ɔ autonomy was in a final sense independent, which was the cause of the fragmenting quality of Gnosticism. In contrast, Paul insists that "none of us lives in relation to himself. . . . If we live, we live in relation to the Lord."[15] It is this relationship, rather than any intrinsic quality in humans themselves, that provides the basis of both law and freedom. Pluralism has its ground in the unique form of Lordship exercised by Christ. And this rules out any strategy of conformity.

III

We turn now to the strategies that Paul advises to sustain and protect the tolerant community of faith. Given Paul's starting point in the relationship between believers and Christ, it is understandable that he would have a particular interest in strategies aimed at protecting the integrity of individual believers. This concern surfaced earlier in the Corinthian correspondence, where the issue was somewhat more clear-cut than it is in Romans. As we have already seen, in I Corinthians 8 and 10 Paul took up the question about the training and protection of "conscience" in connection with eating food offered to idols. Although Paul insisted that the weak should act in such a way as to maintain their own integrity, he nevertheless provided a program for the gradual education of their undeveloped consciences. He recommended that they should cease asking about the origin of particular pieces of meat, in regard to whether it had been offered to idols or not. They are advised to eat with thankfulness on the principle that "the earth is the Lord's, and everything in it" (I Cor. 10:26–30). But if someone informs them that the meat was indeed offered to idols, they are to abstain. Paul's strategy here was brilliant from the educational point of view, based on a grasp of the dynamics of the conscience that seems almost to presuppose the insights of modern depth psychology. Paul's aim was to protect the integrity of the weak, to provide a basis for growth that was not destructive to their moral capacity. His strategy also protects the integrity of the strong. But the difference between Corinthians and Romans at this point is really quite substantial. Whereas Paul developed a plan in Corinthians to gradually overcome elements of pluralism, his program in Rome is to allow that pluralism to stand on a permanent basis.

I believe that the situation Paul faced in Corinth provided the raw materials out of which he could forge his more mature strategies for toleration in a pluralistic church such as that in Rome. These strategies can be broken down into three general categories.

1. The first strategy for toleration in a pluralistic church is protecting the integrity of one's adversaries. This is very prominent in Rom. 14:13–23. Since the danger of the conservatives violating their standards is so clearly stated in the passage, most interpreters fail to see that in fact the integrity of both sides is in view. As Cranfield has shown, the admonition to avoid "judging" is actually broadened somewhat in these verses. Whereas at first (14:3–4, 10) the admonition refers to the action of the weak, it is later extended (14:13b, 14–15) to include the strong.[16] In fact, as Michel observes, the primary target in these verses be-

comes the liberals, who are asked to hold back in their exercise of freedom from the law in order to protect the integrity of the conservatives.[17] A "stumbling block" (14:13, 20) or "stumbling" (14:21) occurs when a conservative is induced to act on a principle of freedom that he or she has not adequately internalized. It represents the violation of integrity, a situation where one is expected to act on the basis of someone else's standards rather than one's own. In the situation at Rome this was the peculiar danger for conservatives, so their adversaries are requested in these verses to act in such a way as to encourage them to avoid such a danger.

The opposite risk is alluded to in Paul's inclusive formula of Rom. 14:13b, where his readers are advised "never to place a stumbling block *or a hindrance* before a brother." Some commentators have felt this double reference was a tautology.[18] But I am inclined to follow Murray in seeing here an allusion to the conservatives enticing the liberals to give up their principles, thus hindering their freedom in the gospel.[19] What Paul has in mind is the insistence on the part of conservatives that liberals should abide by stricter standards than their conscience actually required. It is the problem of reverse discrimination that Paul has in view here. Just as liberals should avoid putting pressure on conservatives to act with more freedom than their conscience allows, so conservatives should avoid pressuring liberals into accepting more restrictive standards.

Each side has the obligation to see that the other side lives up to its own standards, rather than submitting to alien norms. What is so striking about this argument is that the variety in ethical standards within the Roman house churches is admitted as legitimate and the integrity of both sides is viewed as requiring defense. This perspective appears congruent with Jack Pressau's insistence that ministers should avoid imposing "higher levels" of faith and practice than persons in their congregations are able to absorb. "One of the laws of moral development is that people can understand and discuss one stage of moral reasoning *above* where they currently behave. . . . However, there appears to be some element of threat in doing this."[20] Pressau is convinced that each stage has a legitimate form of Christian theology and ethics, and that the tendency to feel superior about being on higher stages of development should be resisted. "Every stage has natural hangups or predispositions to sin built into it,"[21] he writes, so there is a need for mutual responsibility.

Paul's concern that each group should support the moral consistency of the other side is particularly clear in Rom. 14:14–16. If the conservatives are pressured into eating food they are convinced is "common" or nonkosher, they are "grieved" and "ruined" (14:15) through conscience violations. In such a situation even the integrity of liberals is impaired because "what is good" to them, namely their freedom from the law, is "blasphemed." It is discredited because of the harmful effects it has had on others and thus is in danger of not being followed by the liberals themselves. How can one continue to maintain a norm if it proves dangerous to fellow members of the church? Both sides, in effect, are requested to give each other room for the exercise of personal integrity. Paul's argument at this point is similar to what Martin Buber called "primal setting at a distance." Buber writes that "man as man, sets man at a distance and makes him independent; he lets the life of man like himself go on around about him."[22] Genuine relationships require that we refrain from imposing ourselves or our standards on each other, so that we respect the integrity of each person.

The examples of protecting the integrity of one's adversaries in Rom. 14:13–23 provide the key to Paul's inclusive formulation of the ethic of "pleasing the neighbor" in 15:1–2. Without such examples, Paul's admonition could be understood as unprincipled accommodation, acting merely to retain popularity with others. But Paul is conscious of the danger of losing touch with ethical guidelines, as is visible in his insertion of the criterion "for the good" in this verse. To say "let each of us please the neighbor for the good, for the sake of upbuilding" (15:2) means to act in such a way that the exercise of my own standards does not exert pressure on those who prefer alternate standards. The entire argument in this passage, which has developed from Rom. 14:1 on, is presupposed in this particular formulation. The model is pluralism without pressure to conform. To "please" the neighbor in this context is to provide "distance," to use Buber's term. But it does not mean giving up one's own "distance" in the process. To ensure that the guidelines for such risky behavior are plain, Paul goes on to cite the example of Christ (15:3a) and Scripture (15:3b), which is taken as inspired writ to be "our instructor" for the purpose of augmenting maturity and hope (15:4–7).

2. The second strategy for preserving the health of pluralistic communities tends to be overlooked by advocates of accommodating love. Paul insists that protecting the integrity of others should be combined with protecting one's own integrity. This admonition is directed to the conservatives in Rom. 14:14b–23. No matter what principles others, including Paul himself, may follow, food *is* unclean to everyone who thinks it is unclean. So the proper action is that which is consistent with one's own standard. To eat despite the contrary voice of one's own internalized standard is to violate "faith" (14:23) and to fall into self-condemnation (14:22). The connection between this admonition and the principle of an individuated "measuring rod of faith" given to conservatives as well as to liberals was set forth above. To give up such personal integrity under pressure from others is as much a departure from faith as the attempt to impose one's view on others who come from a different tradition.

Although the larger danger of abandoning personal integrity in the Roman church situation was felt on the part of conservatives, Paul explicitly includes the liberals in 14:16. Commentators like Barrett and Käsemann have agreed that it is the "good" freedom of the strong which is in view in the admonition, "Do not let your good be blasphemed."[23] The term *blasphemeō* is used here, in a manner unique to the Pauline letters, to refer not to the scorn of nonbelievers but to the behavior of believers themselves. Paul avoids specifying precisely who does the discrediting in order to convey the sweeping quality of the threat to Christian freedom.[24] If exercised by the strong in an aggressive manner that undermines the integrity of the weak, its damage will appear to be intrinsic to freedom itself. The consequence in such a case would be that Christian freedom, the "good" for which Christ died, would be abandoned as ethically corrosive in a pluralistic setting. Paul's concern that the conservatives avoid providing a "hindrance" to the exercise of freedom is matched here by the admonition to the liberals themselves.

This aspect of Paul's argument could provide a corrective for ethicists concerned to protect the "weak," understood in the modern sense of those lacking willpower to maintain their standards. Particularly in the situation of abstinence from alcohol, the tendency has been to urge those who are free to drink to abstain from the exercise of their freedom in order not to encourage abuse on the part of others. Several factors differentiate this relatively modern interpretation from the Pauline situation. Whereas Paul used "weak" to describe conservatives who were highly bigoted and judgmental, the temperance movement beginning in the last century has tended to think of it as the absence of self-control and willpower. The belief in the inevitability of alcoholism for anybody who takes the first drink, which itself has probably been a powerful encouragement to fatalistic addiction, contrasts with Paul's confidence that either side in Rome could retain their standards and live up to them. This modern tradition has led to a substantial resistance against admitting that the freedom of the strong to partake of any nourishment such as alcohol is intrinsically "good" for them. In fact, as the rhetoric of the prohibition movement has demonstrated, alcohol has been depicted as an absolute evil, as "demon rum." In this case the modern prohibition movement has actually adopted the ethical standard of the conservatives in a place like Rome and has made it normative for all. In effect, the pattern of abstinence and the rationale for the constitutional amendment on this point was to eliminate pluralism in order to defend the conscience of the "weak." It is essential, if the full force of Paul's argument is to be taken, to realize that the integrity of the liberal is as important to preserve as that of the conservative.

3. The third strategy to promote a tolerant pluralism is the encouragement of growth. In place of a strategy that aims at conversion to uniformity of outlook and behavior, Paul advocates here the "edification" of each person in the Christian congregation upon the various foundations provided by a pluralistic faith. The alternative is visible in the exhortation of Rom. 14:19. "Therefore let us pursue the things that make for peace and edifying each other." The aggressive campaigns of the weak and the strong to "judge" and "despise" the others, producing a veritable state of war in the house churches, was to be replaced by "peace." Yet such peace was clearly not to be static, as if either side had a secure corner on the truth and required no further growth. There is a firm insistence here on the need of each side to be edified. Moreover, as Paul formulates it, it is the responsibility of each side to take an active role in the edification of the other. This point is reaffirmed in 15:2, where edification is depicted as the ultimate in "pleasing the neighbor," which is the obligation of "each" Christian. It is the neighbor's edification, not merely one's own, that embodies the internalization of the example of Christ in 15:3. This requires a structure of congregational life that encourages each to be responsible for the growth of others. The mutually nurturing community is thus the ultimate expression of genuine tolerance.

It seems to me that there is an example of this kind of

concern in some of the recent literature on Christian maturity and faith development. Particularly in the work of Douglas E. Wingeier there is an effort to urge that each Christian has the responsibility to become a theologian and that there is a need to "create a climate" that encourages each person to become a fellow pilgrim in the quest for truth, practicing what might be called "church kitchen theology." He writes: "This commitment to quest and dialogue supports the climate of pluralism. . . . We seek to respect the uniqueness of each person's experience and meanings, take scripture and tradition seriously, and learn from each other's insights. . . . The unity of a Christian congregation, however, is not grounded in unanimity but in the covenant with God through Jesus Christ. We belong to one another because we first belong to and have been forgiven by God."[25] Wingeier's point is that the Christian church should respect theological diversity and the freedom of members to do their faith translation, remaining responsible to Scripture, tradition, reason, experience. He goes on to argue in *Working Out Your Own Beliefs* that "the outcome of this corporate effort at doing theology is not conformity, or even full agreement, but rather a sense of commonality in shared meaning. To share meanings is to seek to understand the significance an experience has for someone else, even though it may mean something quite different to me. It is to listen and learn from one another, to support our individual quests for meaning, and to celebrate the discoveries we make along the way."[26]

Paul's emphasis on maturation rests on theoretical foundations visible in his other letters and explicitly stated in Rom. 12:2. The major themes are nonconformity to the world, transformation through the renewal of the mind, and the activation of individual moral discernment, so that each Christian "proves" for himself or herself what is the "will of God." The assumption of the Pauline ethic of maturation is that each person is set free for growth by the "mercies of God" and that growth is integrally related to the joyful response of presenting the whole self as a "living and holy sacrifice, acceptable to God" (Rom. 12:1). Only those whose security and self-identity are fundamentally grounded in unconditional grace are free enough to undergo such constant maturation. Released from the need to conform or to enforce conformity upon others, they present their modest gifts, accomplishments and bodies to God and allow them to be consumed as offerings. And yet, as Rom. 12:3 has laid down, each person retains the standard of the relationship called faith that has been given to him or her. Two of the most important prerequisites for genuine growth are provided here: freedom to change and courage to continue building on the foundation already provided. Once again, these motifs appear in the thought of Douglas E. Wingeier concerning "church kitchen theology," in which he urges that the task of the church is to encourage every Christian to become a theologian, to build on the foundations that each one uniquely has been given.

Two other references in Paul's discussion provide the horizon for this emphasis on the mutually nurturing community. In Rom. 14:17, Paul provides a theological explanation for avoiding the exercise of freedom when it causes others to stumble. "The kingdom of God is not food or drink but righteousness and peace and joy in the Holy Spirit." The progression is logical, for righteousness in Romans denotes the divine power that regains control over disobedient and competitive creatures by means of the gospel. When this transforming encounter between the righteousness of God and the faith of an individual believer occurs, the conflicts between groups like the weak and the strong give way to peace that transcends yet retains the distinctive features of such groups. When this occurs, the source of joy is radically altered. It is no longer joy in one's freedom from the law and one's resultant superiority over others, as in the case of the liberals in Rome. Nor is it the joy in knowing and conforming to an ethical and liturgical code that makes one superior to others, as the conservatives claimed. Rather, it is "joy in the Holy Spirit," the ever-new and transcendent delight in a new relationship with God that makes genuine tolerance of others possible.

The promise of sustenance in this firm relationship with God is conveyed in the summarizing benediction of Rom. 15:5–6. Here the "God of steadfastness and encouragement," who sustains the growth of each member of the community, is said to provide the "same mind" to each member of the community. As defined in Rom. 12:3 and 16 and Rom. 14:1 to 15:4, this expression does not refer to uniformity. Being of "the same mind" has to do with being true to the distinctive "measuring rod of faith" that each person is given in Christ. It involves following the admonitions about mutual edification and concentrating one's joy in healthy and noncompetitive avenues. The purpose is to "praise God with one voice," which means that the unifying factor is the proper relationship to the Transcendent One who remains far above the reach of liberals or conservatives, Greeks or Jews, slaves or free. Whenever this occurs, the mission of the gospel has manifested the "power of God" to triumph over human sin. And tolerance is renewed by the only force that can ultimately sustain it in a pluralistic world—God himself.

Conclusion

TOLERANCE AND MISSION

Paul does not approach tolerance in Romans as an end in itself. It serves the larger purpose of world mission. Paul's thesis in Romans about the gospel as "the power of God for salvation to everyone who has faith, to the Jew first and also to the Greek" (Rom. 1:16) achieves its goal at the conclusion of the discussion of tolerance in Rom. 15:7–13. The verse that opened our discussion of tolerance in Chapter I—"Welcome one another, therefore, as Christ has welcomed you, for the glory of God" (15:7)—leads into an exposition of the relation between mutual acceptance and the hope of the Christian mission to all nations (15:8–13). It is a relation that is not always understood, for it counters widely held assumptions about missionizing. To become tolerant is usually to cease missionizing, and the most vociferous exponents of evangelism are frequently the fanatically narrow-minded. How could Paul have possibly believed that tolerant relations between factions in the church would contribute to the global triumph of "the righteousness of God" (Rom. 1:17)? And even if he committed such an idea to writing in Romans, what possible bearing could it have for our altered circumstances today?

There are a number of indications that churches renowned for their tolerance are declining in membership and outreach and that those with opposite reputations are growing. Several years ago Dean M. Kelley wrote *Why*

Conservative Churches Are Growing, in which he shows
how adherents of such churches develop social coherence
and purpose that translates into growth.[1] Kelley recognizes
the challenge to religious liberty that fiercely partisan
groups pose, but he insists that the benefits they provide to
society justify society's continued toleration of them. The
results of some of the strictest sects are "lives restored to
self-respect, peaceableness, and self-discipline, families
recovered for stability and self-determination, whole com-
panies of men and women bound together and lifted up out
of despair into mutual regard and reinforcement in the
practice of meaningful, purposeful living."[2] Since such
churches are not only growing but also having positive
effects in many instances, it seems inappropriate to view
them as enemies either of tolerance or of the Christian
mission itself.

It is at this point that Paul's approach to tolerance in
Romans has a particular bearing. It counters the tendency
to identify the cause of tolerance with either the conservatives or the liberals. Paul's counsel to the competing factions in Rome was for each to admit the legitimacy of the
other side and to take responsibility for the other's edification. By centering on their relation with the Lord who
stands above every party and race, they would find a new
basis of unity and mission. Rather than devoting their
energies to undercutting and destroying each other, they
should unite in the praise of God, in which they will one
day be joined by all the nations on earth.

This explains why Paul was able to achieve so innovative
a fusion between tolerance and mission. The entire letter to
the Romans served a missionary purpose, as Nils A. Dahl
reminds us.[3] By transcending the tensions between Greeks
and Jews, the gospel reaches out to include the entire
human race. The final purpose of Christ's life and death and
resurrection, according to the missionary theology at the
end of Romans, was "that the Gentiles might glorify God for
his mercy" (Rom. 15:9). The inclusive thrust of this argu-

ment was captured by Paul S. Minear: "All the walls of human separateness and seclusion, of pride and righteousness, of wisdom and power, were forever levelled. . . . Thus the breaking down of all distinctions among men was the manner in which God opened the kingdom to all men."[4] Paul's hope in writing Romans was that the distinctive strengths of the conservatives as well as the liberals would embody this unity by joining in the mission to Spain. Indeed, the mission would be more likely to succeed if both took part, because the intellectual and spiritual resources of one would complement those of the other. To use the terminology of the "faith development" movement, persons on various levels of cognitive and moral development need appropriate forms of religious faith in order to move toward maturity.

The contrast between Paul's approach and the one traditionally followed by conservative as well as liberal churches is sharpened by the insight of Paul Minear concerning the prior history of missionizing:

> We should never forget that Judaism was a missionary religion, that Pharisaism was the spearhead of that mission, and that Paul was foremost among the Pharisees. And as a Pharisee his motivation is both intelligible and respectable, for it is found in many religions. In fact, it is widespread among Christians today. As it is difficult for a man to be a good man without becoming a Pharisee, it is even more difficult for a good man to be a missionary without becoming a Pharisee, and I use the term Pharisee not as a symbol of what was bad in Judaism but of what was good. Yet it was precisely his career as a Pharisee which Paul completely repudiated when Christ called him to a new mission.[5]

The strategy of Pharisaism was to teach and enforce conformity with the law as the means of world redemption. In effect it required the eradication of alien laws and customs, and, in the final step of circumcision, the incorporation of alien races into the very seed of Abraham. The ferocious zeal that marked Paul's participation in this kind of mission

(Gal. 1:13–14) rested on the premise that his theology was ultimate and, consequently, that those who did not agree with it deserved to die. What he discovered on the Damascus road in the encounter with the risen Lord was that his missionary zeal had in fact been at odds with God and that the very outsiders excluded by his former message should now receive the good news of their inclusion. Hence the mission to proclaim the gospel of infinite grace to the Gentiles was given simultaneously with his call to Christian discipleship (Gal. 1:15; Rom. 1:1).

The final issue in the Christian faith is the inclusion of the entire human race, which is something quite different from the success and the growth of conservative or liberal theologies. Although Paul makes it clear in Rom. 14:14; 15:1, and elsewhere that he belonged to the liberal party in early Christianity, he refrains from identifying the triumph of that party with the triumph of the world mission. For the mission to succeed, he insists, there is a need for groups and persons to retain the integrity of their particular ideologies and mores while cooperating in tolerance with their competitors. The good news that finally transforms the world is that God has called conservatives as well as liberals, rich as well as poor, Europeans as well as Asians, Americans as well as Africans to live in praise of his mercies. In this regard, I believe that James W. Fowler is close to the Pauline thesis when he says: "The real question is, will there be *faith* on earth and will it be *good* faith—faith sufficiently inclusive so as to counter and transcend the destructive henotheistic idolatries of national, ethnic, racial and religious identifications and bind us as a human community in convenantal trust and loyalty to each other and to the Ground of our Being?"[6] This does not mean that the debate over the adequate expression of faith should come to an end or that the struggles between factions and nations should be magically quelled. But it does imply that the basis for our unity is faith in the God who both transcends and values us, the one who revealed his essential nature and will in the life and death of Jesus Christ, and who calls us to extend the kind of tolerance to each other that we have already received in him.

To proclaim such a faith as this would mean to counter the ground swell of racism and violence that now threatens the future of our planet. It calls us to set our confidence not in the superiority of our views or our arms but rather in the power of the gospel to work its transforming miracle, first with us and then with all others who require a new basis for knowing that they are sons and daughters of a tolerant parent. The words from Isaiah that Paul selected to climax his fusion of tolerance and mission seem to be appropriate for us as well:

> The root of Jesse shall come,
> he who rises to rule the Gentiles;
> in him shall the Gentiles hope.
> (Rom. 15:12)

NOTES

Introduction
THE DILEMMA OF TOLERANCE TODAY

1. *Sunday Journal and Star* (Lincoln, Neb.; Oct. 25, 1981), p. F1.
2. Bruce Buursma, "Religion's Turn to Right Nothing New," *Chicago Tribune* (Jan. 5, 1981), p. 4.
3. Robert Paul Wolff, *The Poverty of Liberalism* (Beacon Press, 1968); Robert Paul Wolff, Barrington Moore, Jr., and Herbert Marcuse, *A Critique of Pure Tolerance* (Beacon Press, 1965).
4. John Murray Cuddihy, *No Offense: Civil Religion and Protestant Taste* (Seabury Press, A Crossroad Book, 1978).
5. *Soundings: An Interdisciplinary Journal*, Vol. 61 (1978), p. 229.
6. Robert Bellah, "Commentary and Proposed Agenda: The Normative Framework for Pluralism in America," *Soundings*, Vol. 61 (1978), p. 371.
7. Martin E. Marty, *The Public Church: Mainline-Evangelical-Catholic* (Crossroad Publishing Co., 1981), p. 135.
8. Ernst Käsemann, *Jesus Means Freedom*, tr. by Frank Clarke (Fortress Press, 1970); Hans-Werner Bartsch, "Die Idee der Toleranz bei Paulus," *Kerygma und Mythos*, Vol. VI-5 (Hamburg: Herbert Reich, 1974), pp. 163–167.

Chapter I
STRENUOUS TOLERANCE FLOWING FROM VITAL FAITH

1. Carl Schneider, "Ursprung und Ursachen der christlichen Intoleranz," *Zeitschrift für Religions- und Geistesgeschichte*, Vol. 30 (1978), p. 203.
2. Ibid., p. 211.

3. Bartsch, "Die Idee der Toleranz bei Paulus," *Kerygma und Mythos*, Vol. VI-5, pp. 163–167.

4. John Howard Schütz, *Paul and the Anatomy of Apostolic Authority* (Cambridge University Press, 1975); Bengt Holmberg, *Paul and Power: The Structure of Authority in the Primitive Church as Reflected in the Pauline Epistles* (Fortress Press, 1980).

5. Robert Jewett, "The Redaction and the I Corinthians and the Trajectory of the Pauline School," *Journal of the American Academy of Religion Supplement*, Vol. 46 (1978), pp. 400–409.

6. In "The Sexual Liberation of the Apostle Paul," *Journal of the American Academy of Religion Supplement*, Vol. 47 (1979), pp. 55–87, I summarize the scholarship on this issue, with particular reference to Johannes Weiss, *Der erste Korintherbrief* (Göttingen: Vandenhoeck & Ruprecht, 1910) and Gottfried Fitzer, *"Das Weib schweige in der Gemeinde." Über den unpaulinischen Charakter der mulier-taceat-Verse in 1. Korinther 14* (Munich: Chr. Kaiser, 1963).

7. Walter Schmithals, *Paul and the Gnostics*, tr. by John E. Steely (Abingdon Press, 1972), pp. 219–238. He expanded his view to account for the entirety of Rom. 16:1–20 as a letter to Ephesus in *Der Römerbrief als historisches Problem* (Gütersloh: Gerd Mohn, 1975), pp. 125–151. I no longer find the arguments for the Ephesian provenance of Romans 16 plausible, but the case Schmithals has made concerning vs. 17–20 remains convincing.

8. John Knox, "The Epistle to the Romans," *The Interpreter's Bible*, Vol. 9 (Abingdon Press, 1954), p. 664.

9. Walter Bauer, *A Greek-English Lexicon of the New Testament and Other Early Christian Literature*, tr. and adapted by William F. Arndt, F. Wilbur Gingrich, and Frederick W. Danker (University of Chicago Press, 1979), p. 764.

10. Cf. *Report of the Synodical President to the Lutheran Church—Missouri Synod* (Sept. 1, 1972), p. 4 : "A study of the history of The Lutheran Church—Missouri Synod will reveal that the Synod has always been concerned about its doctrine. Indeed, the Constitution of the Synod ... lists as the first object of the Synod: 'The conservation and promotion of the unity of the true faith (Eph. 4:3–6; I Cor. 1:10) and a united defense against schism and sectarianism (Rom. 16:17).' " There are frequent references to this verse in Romans in the congregational resolutions printed in the Missouri Synod's *Convention Workbook (Reports and Overtures)*, particularly in resolutions against pulpit and altar fellowship with other Lutheran denominations.

11. Cf. Robert Jewett, "Conflicting Movements in the Early Church as Reflected in Philippians," *Novum Testamentum*, Vol. 12 (1970), pp. 363–390.

12. Ernst Käsemann, *Commentary on Romans,* tr. and ed. by G. W. Bromiley (Wm. B. Eerdmans Publishing Co., 1980), p. 418.

13. Cited from George F. Forell (ed.), *Christian Social Teachings* (Doubleday & Co., 1966), p. 205.

14. Robert Jewett, "The Form and Function of the Homiletic Benediction," *Anglican Theological Review,* Vol. 6 (1969), pp. 18–34.

15. Cf. Käsemann, *Romans,* p. 418.

16. Käsemann, *Romans,* p. 364; Otto Michel, *Der Brief an die Römer,* 12th edition (Göttingen: Vandenhoeck & Ruprecht, 1963), p. 333; Knox, "Romans," p. 613; C. K. Barrett, *A Commentary on the Epistle to the Romans* (Harper & Brothers, 1958), p. 256.

17. Wilhelm Wuellner, "Paul's Rhetoric of Argumentation in Romans: An Alternative to the Donfried-Karris Debate Over Romans," in *The Romans Debate,* ed. by Karl P. Donfried (Augsburg Publishing House, 1977), p. 171.

18. Ernest Findlay Scott, *Paul's Epistle to the Romans* (London: SCM Press, 1947), p. 72.

19. Ibid., p. 73.

20. Werner G. Kümmel, *Introduction to the New Testament,* tr. by A. T. Mattill, Jr. (Abingdon Press, 1966), p. 221. This is a view I accepted at the time of writing *Paul's Anthropological Terms: A Study of Their Use in Conflict Settings* (Leiden: E. J. Brill, 1971); see p. 47.

21. Wuellner, "Paul's Rhetoric," pp. 165–174.

22. Robert Jewett, "Romans as an Ambassadorial Letter," forthcoming in *Interpretation* (1982).

23. Karl P. Donfried, "False Presuppositions in the Study of Romans," in Donfried (ed.), *The Romans Debate,* p. 122.

24. My views on this topic have had to be altered under the impact of studies by Kurt Aland, "Der Schluss und die ursprüngliche Gestalt des Römerbriefes," *Neutestamentliche Entwürfe* (Munich: Chr. Kaiser, 1979), pp. 284–301, and Harry Y. Gamble, *The Textual History of the Letter to the Romans* (Wm. B. Eerdmans Publishing Co., 1977).

25. Cf. Wolfgang Wiefel, "The Jewish Community in Ancient Rome and the Origins of Roman Christianity," in Donfried (ed.), *The Romans Debate,* pp. 105–113.

26. Rom. 16:5 refers to the "church" in the house of Prisca and Aquila; 16:10 refers to "those belonging to Aristobulus," probably a reference to a section of the imperial bureaucracy called the Aristobuliani; 16:11 refers to "those belonging to Narcissus," probably a reference to another section of the imperial bureaucracy called the Narcissiani; 16:14 refers to "the brethren" with Asyncritus, Phlegon, and others; and 16:15 refers to "all the

saints" with Philologus, Julia, and others. J. B. Lightfoot (ed.), in *Saint Paul's Epistle to the Philippians* (London: Macmillan & Co., 1900; Grand Rapids: Zondervan Publishing House, 1957), set forth the evidence concerning these five house churches (pp. 174f.) in a manner that has convinced more recent exegetes such as Michel (*Römer*, p. 380) and C. E. B. Cranfield (*The Epistle to the Romans;* 2 vols., Edinburgh: T. & T. Clark, 1975–79, pp. 786–795).

27. This view is compatible with that stated by William S. Campbell, "Why Did Paul Write Romans?" *Expository Times,* Vol. 85 (1974), pp. 268f., and idem, "Romans III as a Key to the Structure and Thought of the Letter," *Novum Testamentum,* Vol. 23 (1981), pp. 22–40.

28. Wiefel, "Roman Christianity," pp. 100–119.

29. Ibid., p. 108.

30. Ibid., p. 109.

31. Paul S. Minear, *The Obedience of Faith: The Purposes of Paul in the Epistle to the Romans* (London: SCM Press, 1971), p. 11.

32. Cf. Wiefel, "Roman Christianity," pp. 115–119; George La Piana, "Foreign Groups in Rome During the First Centuries of the Empire," *Harvard Theological Review,* Vol. 20 (1927), pp. 341–393.

33. Hans-Werner Bartsch, "Die historische Situation des Römerbriefes," *Texte und Untersuchungen,* Vol. 102 (1968), pp. 281–291; idem, "Die antisemitischen Gegner des Paulus im Römerbrief," in *Antijudaismus im Neuen Testament,* ed. by W. P. Eckert et al. (Munich: Chr. Kaiser, 1967), pp. 27–43; G. Harder, "Der konkrete Anlass des Römerbriefes," *Theologia Viatorum,* Vol. 6 (1959), pp. 13–24; William S. Campbell, "The Place of Romans 9–11 Within the Structure and Thought of the Letter," *Texte und Untersuchungen (Studia Evangelica)* (1981), pp. 120–130; Bruce Corley, "The Jews, the Future and God (Rom. 9–11)," *Southwestern Journal of Theology,* Vol. 19 (1976), pp. 42–56; Dieter Zeller, *Juden und Heiden in der Mission des Paulus: Studien zum Römerbrief* (Stuttgart: Katholisches Bibelwerk, 1973).

34. Cf. Lightfoot, *Philippians,* pp. 174f.

35. Wiefel, "Roman Christianity," p. 113.

36. Ernest Best, *The Letter of Paul to the Romans* (Cambridge University Press, 1967), p. 163.

37. Cf. Cranfield, *Romans,* p. 700; Michel, *Römer,* pp. 334–350; Wilhelm Lütgert, "Der Römerbrief als historisches Problem," *Beiträge zur Förderung christlicher Theologie,* Vol. 17 (1913), pp. 31–140; Max Rauer, "Die 'Schwachen' in Korinth und Rom," *Biblische Studien,* Vol. 21 (1923), pp. 1–192.

38. I agree with Käsemann (*Romans*, p. 353), as against Cranfield and others, that "him'" at the end of Rom. 14:3 refers in principle to both the weak and the strong. Although it is a singular, its sense in the context of this argument is inclusive.

39. Cf. Michel, *Römer*, p. 338.

40. Raoul Dederen, "On Esteeming One Day Better than Another," *Andrews University Seminary Studies*, Vol. 9 (1971), p. 23.

41. Ibid., p. 27.

42. Käsemann, *Romans*, p. 371.

43. Cf. Michel, *Römer*, pp. 295f. and 307, for his discussion of Rom. 12:3 and 12:16.

44. Frédéric Godet, *Commentary on St. Paul's Epistle to the Romans*, tr. by A. Cusin and T. W. Chambers (Funk & Wagnalls, 1883).

45. Gustav Mensching, *Tolerance and Truth in Religion*, tr. by H.-J. Klimkeit (University of Alabama Press, 1971), pp. 11–99.

46. Ibid., p. 148.

47. Glenn Tinder, *Tolerance: Toward a New Civility* (University of Massachusetts Press, 1976), p. 81.

48. Ibid., p. 139.

49. Ibid., p. 138.

50. Käsemann, *Romans*, p. 385; Cranfield, *Romans*, p. 739.

51. Knox, *Romans*, pp. 637f.

52. Ulrich Wilckens, *Der Brief an die Römer* (Zurich: Benzinger; Neukirchen: Neukirchener Verlag, 1978–79), Vol. I, p. 199.

53. Cuddihy, *No Offense*, pp. 4–6.

54. Cited by Laurence J. Peter, *Peter's Quotations: Ideas for Our Time* (William Morrow & Co., 1977), p. 471.

55. Harry Emerson Fosdick, *Adventurous Religion and Other Essays* (Harper & Brothers, 1926), p. 225.

56. Gordon Allport, *The Nature of Prejudice* (Doubleday & Co., Anchor Books, 1958), pp. 399f.

57. Mensching, *Tolerance*, p. 79.

58. Ibid., p. 82.

59. "Christ, from Whom All Blessings Flow," *The Methodist Hymnal* (Methodist Publishing House, 1966), p. 530.

60. Ernst Kühl, *Der Brief des Paulus an die Römer* (Leipzig: Quelle & Meyer, 1913), p. 464; my translation.

61. Godet, *Romans*, p. 470.

62. Cf. Robert Jewett, *The Captain America Complex: The Dilemma of Zealous Nationalism* (Westminster Press, 1973), pp. 35–37.

63. Cf. Robert Jewett and John Shelton Lawrence, *The Ameri-*

can Monomyth (Doubleday & Co., Anchor Press Book, 1977).

64. Samuel Terrien, *The Elusive Presence: Toward a New Biblical Theology* (Harper & Row, Publishers, 1978).

Chapter II
CONSCIENCE AND THE MEASURING ROD OF FAITH

1. Roland H. Bainton, *The Travail of Religious Liberty: Nine Biographical Studies* (Westminster Press, 1951), pp. 119f.

2. The Meadville/Lombard Theological School Dissertation of 1980 by Jay Atkinson, *Religious Tolerance in Unitarian Universalism: Stalking the Elusive Virtue,* summarizes the scholarly opinion on this point, noting that Castellio explicitly cited Jesus in *Conseil de la France desolée* (Repr.; Geneva: Librairie Droz, 1967), p. 26. There is, however, in Joseph Lecler's *Toleration and the Reformation,* tr. by T. L. Westow (2 vols., Association Press, 1960), Vol. I, p. 342, a reference to Castellio's citation of Rom. 14:3 in defense of Christians not condemning each other.

3. Werner Kaegi, *Castellio und die Anfänge der Toleranz* (Basel: Halbing & Lichtenhahn, 1953), pp. 18f.

4. Bainton, *The Travail of Religious Liberty,* p. 221.

5. *Letters of Roger Williams,* ed. by J. R. Bartlett (Providence: Narragansett Club, 1874), Vol. 6, p. 219.

6. Ibid, p. 225.

7. Cf. the history of research on "conscience" in Jewett, *Paul's Anthropological Terms,* pp. 402–420, and my article entitled "Conscience" in *The Interpreter's Dictionary of the Bible, Supplementary Volume,* ed. by K. Crim et al. (Abingdon Press, 1976), pp. 173–174.

8. Lecler discusses the controversy between the Thomists and the Augustinians on the issue of conscience. St. Thomas maintained that conscience was binding even when in error. However, he conceded that if there was a clear moral law on the issue, conscience must be set aside. "In practice, then, St. Thomas does not go beyond the conclusions of the Augustinian school. If one sins by acting against an erroneous conscience, one sins also by following it. . . . The only remedy is to put such a conscience aside, doubtless by recourse to the advice of those who know and to prayer" (*Toleration and the Reformation,* Vol. I, p. 99).

9. This analysis rests on a partition theory worked out in my "The Redaction of I Corinthians and the Trajectory of the Pauline School," *Journal of the American Academy of Religion, Supplement 46* (1978), pp. 389–404. Letter A consists of I Cor. 11:2–34; Letter B contains II Cor. 6:14 to 7:1 + I Cor. 6:12–20 + I Cor. 9:24 to 10:22 + I Cor. 15:1–58 + I Cor. 16:13–24; Letter C contains I

Cor. 1:1 to 6:11 + I Cor. 7:1 to 8:13 + I Cor. 9:19–23 + I Cor. 10:23 to 11:1 + I Cor. 12:1–31a + I Cor. 14:1c–40 + I Cor. 12:31b to 13:13 + I Cor. 16:1–12; Letter D contains II Cor. 2:14 to 6:13 + II Cor. 7:2–4; Letter E contains II Cor. 10:1 to 12:13 + I Cor. 9:1–18 + II Cor. 12:14 to 13:13; Letter F consists of II Cor. 9:1–15; and Letter G contains II Cor. 1:1 to 2:13 + II Cor. 7:5 to 8:24.

10. Cf. Walter Schmithals, *Gnosticism in Corinth*, tr. by John E. Steely (Abingdon Press, 1971), pp. 141ff.; Ulrich Wilckens, *Weisheit und Torheit* (Tübingen: J. C. B. Mohr, 1959), pp. 11ff.

11. Cf. C. F. G. Heinrici, *Kritisch-exegetisches Handbuch über den ersten Brief an die Korinther* (Göttingen: Vandenhoeck & Ruprecht, 1888), which provides a list of earlier scholars holding this view on p. 238; it was stated in classic form by Johannes Weiss, *Der erste Korintherbrief* (Göttingen: Vandenhoeck & Ruprecht, 10th ed., 1925), p. 230.

12. Rudolf Bultmann holds the opposite view: "that conscience means self's knowledge of itself ... in responsibility to the transcendent power [of God]" (*Theology of the New Testament*, tr. by K. Grobel; 2 vols., London: SCM Press, 1952–56; Vol. I, p. 220).

13. Weiss, *Der erste Korintherbrief*, p. 265.

14. C. A. Pierce, *Conscience in the New Testament* (London: SCM Press, 1955), p. 62.

15. Cf. Hans Lietzmann, *An die Korinther I–II* (Tübingen: J. C. B. Mohr, 2d ed., 1923), p. 52.

16. Cf. James Moffatt, *The First Epistle of Paul to the Corinthians* (London: Hodder & Stoughton, 1954), p. 144; Jean Héring, *La Première Épître de Saint Paul aux Corinthiens* (Neuchâtel: Delachaux et Niestlé, 1949), p. 99.

17. Cf. Archibald Robertson and Alfred Plummer, *A Critical and Exegetical Commentary on the First Epistle of St. Paul to the Corinthians* (Edinburgh: T. & T. Clark, 2d ed., 1914), pp. 222–223; E.-B. Allo, *Première Épître aux Corinthiens* (Paris: J. Gabalda, 2d ed., 1956), p. 99.

18. Cf. Weiss, *Der erste Korintherbrief*, p. 266.

19. This is the view taken by Pierce, that conscience in this verse is the "pain consequent upon committing the (supposedly) wrong act." By translating *hupo* in the odd sense of "of," he renders the sentence in a virtually nonsensical manner: "Why is my liberty judged of another's conscience?" (*Conscience*, p. 78).

20. Cf. Max Rauer, "Die 'Schwachen' in Korinth und Rom," pp. 1–192.

21. See Walther Eichrodt, *Theology of the Old Testament*, tr. by J. A. Baker (2 vols., Westminster Press, 1961, 1967), Vol. II, pp. 147–150.

22. Cf. also II Cor. 1:12 and my discussion of the issue in *Paul's*

Anthropological Terms, pp. 441–446.

23. Christian Maurer, "*Sunoida*, etc.," in Gerhard Kittel and Gerhard Friedrich (eds.), *Theological Dictionary of the New Testament* (Wm. B. Eerdmans Publishing Co., 1964–76), Vol. 7, pp. 898–919. (Hereafter cited as *TDNT*.)

24. Cf. Jewett, *Paul's Anthropological Terms*, pp. 442f.

25. Cf. Günther Bornkamm, *Studien zur Antike und Urchristentum* (Munich: Chr. Kaiser, 1959), p. 112.

26. Adolf Schlatter, *Gottes Gerechtigkeit: Ein Kommentar zum Römerbrief* (Stuttgart: W. Kohlhammer, 1935), p. 92; translation mine.

27. Cf. Jewett, *Paul's Anthropological Terms*, p. 445.

28. Maurer, "*Sunoida*, etc.," *TDNT*, Vol. 7, p. 916.

29. Paraphrased from Jewett, *Paul's Anthropological Terms*, p. 446.

30. Cf. Theodor Zahn, *Der Brief des Paulus an die Römer* (Leipzig: Deichert, 1910), p. 429.

31. Maurer, "*Sunoida*, etc.," *TDNT*, Vol. 7, p. 916.

32. Cf. Michel, *Römer*, p. 224.

33. Nils Alstrup Dahl and Paul Donahue, *Studies in Paul: Theology for the Early Christian Mission* (Augsburg Publishing House, 1977), pp. 139–142.

34. Paraphrased from Jewett, *Paul's Anthropological Terms*, p. 446.

35. Cf. also the article by W. Magass, "Die Paradigmatik einer Paränese am Beispiel von Röm 12,3: 'er soll nicht höher von sich denken, als er denken darf.' Ein Beitrag zum Häresieverdacht als Terma-Verdacht," *Linguistica Biblica*, Vol. 35 (1975), pp. 1–26.

36. Helen North, *Sophrosyne: Self-Knowledge and Self-Restraint in Greek Literature* (Cornell University Press, 1966).

37. Johanna Schmidt, "Metron ariston—Mass und Harmonie: Hellenistischer Ursprung einer abendländischen Ideologie," *Epistēmonikē Epetēris tēs philosophikēs Scholēs tou panepistēmiou Athēnōn*, Vol. 15 (1964–65), pp. 514–563.

38. Hans Dieter Betz, *Der Apostel Paulus und die sokratische Tradition* (Tübingen: J. C. B. Mohr [Paul Siebeck], 1972), pp. 130f.

39. F. F. Bruce, *The Epistle of Paul to the Romans: An Introduction and Commentary* (London: Inter-Varsity Press, 1963), p. 227; cf. also Barrett, *Romans*, p. 235.

40. Cranfield, *Romans*, p. 614.

41. Idem.

42. Cf. Bauer, *Lexicon*, "*metron*," p. 504, which places Rom. 12:3 under the category of "deal out, assign, apportion something to someone."

43. Ibid., p. 515.

44. Glenn E. Tinder, *The Crisis of Political Imagination* (Charles Scribner's Sons, 1964), p. 270.

45. H. A. W. Meyer, *Critical and Exegetical Handbook to the Epistle to the Romans*, tr. by J. C. Moore (Edinburgh: T. & T. Clark, 1876), Vol. II, p. 322.

46. W. E. Vine, *The Epistle to the Romans: Doctrine, Precept, Practice*, rev. ed. (London: Marshall, Morgan & Scott, 1948), p. 204.

47. William Sanday and Arthur C. Headlam, *A Critical and Exegetical Commentary on the Epistle to the Romans* (5th ed., 1895; Alec R. Allenson, 1958), p. 394.

48. Karl Barth, *The Epistle to the Romans*, tr. by E. C. Hoskyns (Oxford University Press, 6th ed., 1933), p. 522.

49. Käsemann, *Romans*, p. 379.

50. Cranfield, *Romans*, p. 726.

51. Best, *Romans*, p. 160; Sanday and Headlam, *Romans*, p. 393.

52. Käsemann (*Romans*, p. 379) refers to E. Gaugler and H. Ridderbos as holding this view.

53. Cranfield, *Romans*, p. 726.

54. Barrett, *Romans*, p. 266.

55. In Bauer, *Lexicon*, this is described at *"kata,"* under category 5a, p. 407.

56. Hans-Werner Bartsch, "The Concept of Faith in Paul's Letter to the Romans," *Biblical Research*, Vol. 13 (1968), p. 45.

57. The hypothesis is spelled out in detail in *Interpretation* (Jan. 1981).

Chapter III
FAITH WITHOUT TOLERANCE AND TOLERANCE WITHOUT FAITH

1. Cf. Meinulf Barbers, *Toleranz bei Sebastian Franck* (Bonn: Ludwig Röhrscheid, 1964).

2. Sébastien Châteillon, *Concerning Heretics*, tr. by R. H. Bainton (Columbia University Press, 1935), pp. 99–101.

3. Tinder, *Tolerance*, p. 87.

4. Ibid., pp. 98–103.

5. Werner H. Schmidt, *Das erste Gebot: Seine Bedeutung für das Alte Testament* (Munich: Chr. Kaiser, 1969), p. 14.

6. Samuel Terrien states the consensus that this was the original form of the Second Commandment, and that the material presently in Ex. 20:4b–6 consists of "catechetic accretions which clearly point to a later age" (*Elusive Presence*, p. 130).

7 Jay G. Williams, *Ten Words of Freedom: An Introduction to*

the Faith of Israel (Fortress Press, 1971), p. 100.

8. Schmidt, *Das erste Gebot,* pp. 18f.

9. Terrien, *Elusive Presence,* p. 201.

10. Schmidt, *Das erste Gebot,* p. 21; translation mine.

11. Williams, *Ten Words of Freedom,* p. 115.

12. Ibid., p. 116.

13. Schmidt, *Das erste Gebot,* p. 47. He refers in a footnote to Hartmut Gese's statement that "the first and second commandments belong together: 'God himself' is the theme" (*Zeitschrift für Theologie und Kirche,* Vol. 64 [1967], p. 132; translation mine).

14. Cranfield, *Romans,* p. 106.

15. Käsemann, *Romans,* p. 38; Wilckens, *Römer,* pp. 104f.

16. Cf. the extensive discussion of the debate over this verse among the church fathers as described by Cranfield, *Romans,* pp. 134f.

17. Dodd, *Romans,* p. 28.

18. Meg Greenfield, "Collapse of Certainty," *Newsweek* (May 21, 1979), p. 104.

19. Peter Shaw, "Degenerate Criticism: The Dismal State of English Studies," *Harper's* (Oct. 1979), p. 93.

20. Ibid., p. 94.

21. Ibid., p. 96.

22. John Gardner, *On Moral Fiction* (Basic Books, 1978), pp. 5f.

23. Ibid., p. 42.

24. This excerpt from Alexander Solzhenitsyn's remarks at Harvard University on the occasion of his honorary doctorate, June 8, 1978, was cited in *Newsweek* (Dec. 25, 1978), p. 72.

25. Käsemann, *Romans,* p. 42.

26. Cranfield, *Romans,* p. 117.

27. Käsemann, *Romans,* p. 44.

28. Cf. Scott, *Romans,* pp. 31f.

29. Peter Shaw, "Degenerate Criticism," p. 93.

30. Benjamin DeMott, "Six Novels in Search of a Novelist," *Atlantic* (Nov. 1979), p. 91.

31. Ibid., p. 92.

32. This remark appeared on a *60 Minutes* television report on Dec. 16, 1979; cf. in this connection Walter Clemons' review of the first volume of Henry Kissinger's memoirs *(The White House Years)* in *Newsweek* (Nov. 12, 1979), pp. 111–112.

33. Käsemann, *Romans,* p. 44.

34. Franz J. Leenhardt, *The Epistle to the Romans: A Commentary,* tr. by Harold Knight (London: Lutterworth Press, 1961), pp. 67f.

35. Peter Shaw, "Degenerate Criticism," p. 93.

36. Käsemann, *Romans,* p. 47.

37. Cf. Michel, *Römer*, pp. 68f.

38. Käsemann, *Romans*, pp. 50, 49.

39. Tinder, *The Crisis of Political Imagination*, pp. 18f.

40. Cf. Émile Durkheim, *The Division of Labor in Society*, tr. by George Simpson (Free Press of Glencoe, 1964), Vol. 3, pp. 353-373; Robert K. Merton, *Social Theory and Social Structure*, rev. ed. (Free Press, 1957).

41. Peter Berger, *The Homeless Mind: Modernization and Consciousness* (Random House, Vintage Books, 1974), pp. 184f.

42. Michel, *Römer*, p. 88.

43. Moffatt, *Romans*, p. 38; Cranfield explicitly rejects this implication of irony in *Romans*, p. 167.

44. Cf. Wilckens, *Römer*, p. 149.

45. Michel, *Römer*, p. 89; Hermann L. Strack and Paul Billerbeck, *Kommentar zum Neuen Testament aus Talmud und Midrasch* (5 vols.; Munich: Beck, 1922–55), Vol. III, pp. 113f.

46. Käsemann, *Romans*, p. 69.

47. Ibid., pp. 102, 104.

48. Martin Hengel, *Die Zeloten* (Leiden: E. J. Brill, 1961); idem, *Victory Over Violence: Jesus and the Revolutionists*, tr. by David E. Green (Fortress Press, 1973); idem, *Was Jesus a Revolutionist?* tr. by W. Klassen (Fortress Press, 1971).

49. Cranfield, *Romans*, p. 514.

50. Cited by Wayne A. Meeks, in Wayne A. Meeks (ed.), *The Writings of St. Paul* (W. W. Norton & Co., 1972), p. 242.

51. Jacob Bronowski, "The Principle of Tolerance," *Atlantic* (Dec. 1973), p. 65.

52. Ibid., p. 59.

53. Ibid., p. 66.

Chapter IV

The Limits of Tolerance

1. Lance Morrow, "Will America Get Over Its Grossness?" *Des Moines Register* (Feb. 27, 1980).

2. Norman Cousins, "The Reign of the Religious Fanatic," *Saturday Review* (Jan. 6, 1979), p. 10.

3. Cf. Cranfield, *Romans*, p. 628; Barrett, *Romans*, pp. 239–243; Charles H. Talbert, "Tradition and Redaction in Romans XII, 9–21," *New Testament Studies*, Vol. 16 (1969), pp. 83–93.

4. Meyer, *Romans*, p. 475.

5. Godet, *Romans*, p. 434.

6. Cf. Dieter Georgi, *Die Gegner des Paulus im 2. Korintherbrief: Studien zur religiösen Propaganda in der Spätantike* (Neukirchen: Neukirchener Verlag, 1964); idem, "Second Letter to the

Corinthians," *The Interpreter's Dictionary of the Bible, Supplementary Volume*, pp. 183–186.

7. Cranfield, *Romans*, pp. 630f.

8. Ulrich Wilckens' article on the Greek term translated "genuine" *(anupokritos)*, in *TDNT*, Vol. 8, pp. 559–571, shows that in pre-Christian usage it did not have the connotation of "sincere" or "unhypocritical" which a number of modern commentators have imposed on it. Thus the term relates more to the publicly tested realm of authenticity than to the private arena of inner motivations.

9. Cf. Roland H. Bainton, *Erasmus of Christendom* (Charles Scribner's Sons, 1969), pp. 184–186.

10. Morrow, "Will America Get Over Its Grossness?"

11. Gardner, *On Moral Fiction*, p. 146.

12. Ibid., p. 175.

13. Tinder, *Tolerance*, p. 161.

14. See *"apostugeō,"* in Henry George Liddell and Robert Scott, *A Greek-English Lexicon*, 9th ed., revised and augmented by H. Stuart Jones and R. McKenzie (Oxford: Clarendon Press, 1940), p. 220. The term is used here for the only time in the entire New Testament.

15. Sanday and Headlam, *Romans*, p. 360.

16. Laurence J. Peter, *Peter's Quotations*, p. 471.

17. Walter Berns, "For Capital Punishment: The Morality of Anger," *Harper's* (April 1979), p. 16.

18. Tinder, *Tolerance*, pp. 158–160.

19. Robert Jewett and John Shelton Lawrence, *The American Monomyth;* idem, "Mythic Conformity in the Cuckoo's Nest," *Psychocultural Review*, Vol. 1 (1977), pp. 68–76; idem, "Beyond the Pornography of Violence," *Religion in Life*, Vol. 46 (1977), pp. 357–363; idem, "Pop Fascism in *Star Wars*—Or Vision of a Better World?" *Des Moines Register* (Nov. 27, 1977); idem, "The Problem of Mythic Imperialism," *Journal of American Culture*, Vol. 2 (1979), pp. 309–320.

20. Cf. Marty, *The Public Church*, pp. 135–137.

21. Gabriel Marcel, *Creative Fidelity*, tr. by Robert Rosthal (Farrar, Straus & Co., 1964), p. 211.

22. The term *kollaō* is discussed by K. L. Schmidt in *TDNT*, Vol. 3, pp. 822f.; cf. also Zahn, *Römer*, p. 548.

23. Werner Jaeger, *Paideia: The Ideals of Greek Culture*, tr. by Gilbert Highet, Vol. II (Oxford University Press, 1943), pp. 189f.

24. Alexander Pope, "An Essay on Criticism" (1711), in *English Literature: A Period Anthology*, ed. by A. E. Baugh and G. W. McClelland (Appleton-Century-Crofts, 1954), p. 587.

25. John Keats, "Endymion" (1817–18), in Baugh and McClel-

land (eds.), *English Literature*, p. 909.

26. Alfred, Lord Tennyson, "In Memoriam A.H.H." (1850), in Baugh and McClelland (eds.), *English Literature*, pp. 1043, 1045.

27. Gardner, *On Moral Fiction*, pp. 133, 146.

28. Bryan F. Griffin, "Panic Among the Philistines," *Harper's* (Aug. & Sept. 1981); Part 2, "The Literary Vulgarians," p. 41.

29. Ibid., p. 54.

30. Bauer, *Lexicon*, p. 712, and Liddell and Scott, *Lexicon*, p. 1480, show that "taking the lead" is the basic meaning of *proēgoumenoi;* Michel, *Römer*, p. 303, provides the references in Hebrew literature for the honorific expression concerning greeting and welcoming others.

31. Cf. Ernst Käsemann, *Perspectives on Paul*, tr. by Margaret Kohl (Fortress Press, 1971), p. 75.

32. Cf. Rom. 15:25f.; I Cor. 16:1, 15; II Cor. 8:4.

33. Cf. David Daube, "Jewish Missionary Maxims in Paul," *Studia Theologica*, Vol. 1 (1948), pp. 158–169; Charles H. Talbert, "Tradition and Redaction in Romans XII, 9–21," *New Testament Studies*, Vol. 16 (1969), pp. 83–93.

34. Cf. Schmithals, *Gnosticism in Corinth*, pp. 182f.; Michel, *Römer*, p. 307.

35. Godet, *Romans*, p. 437.

36. Talbert, "Tradition and Reaction," p. 91.

37. William Klassen, "Coals of Fire: Sign of Repentance or Revenge," *New Testament Studies*, Vol. 9 (1962–63), pp. 337–350.

38. Cf. Kühl, *Römer*, p. 430.

39. Cf. Clinton D. Morrison, *The Powers That Be: Earthly Rulers and Demonic Powers in Romans 13.1–7* (London: SCM Press, 1960); Wolfgang Schrage, *Die Christen und der Staat nach dem Neuen Testament* (Gütersloh: Gerd Mohn, 1971); Ernst Käsemann, "Römer 13, 1–7 in unserer Generation," *Zeitschrift für Theologie und Kirche*, Vol. 56 (1959), pp. 316–376; also Käsemann, "Principles of the Interpretation of Romans 13," in his *New Testament Questions for Today*, tr. by W. J. Montague (Fortress Press, 1969), pp. 196–216.

40. Marcus Borg, "A New Context for Romans XIII," *New Testament Studies*, Vol. 19 (1972–73), pp. 210, 214f.; similar views were developed in the nineteenth century as discussed by Meyer, *Romans*, Vol. II, pp. 275–284.

41. Borg, loc. cit., p. 217.

42. Ibid., p. 218.

43. Johannes Friedrich, Wolf Pöhlmann, and Peter Stuhlmacher, "Zur historischen Situation und Intention von Röm 13, 1–7," *Zeitschrift für Theologie und Kirche*, Vol. 73 (1976), p. 158; the Suetonius reference is in *Nero* 10.

44. Ibid., p. 161; my translation.
45. Cf. Arnaldo Momigliano, "Nero," in *The Cambridge Ancient History,* Vol. 10, p. 720; Brian H. Warmington, *Nero: Reality and Legend* (W. W. Norton & Co., 1970).
46. August Strobel, "Zum Verständnis von Rm 13," *Zeitschrift für die neutestamentliche Wissenschaft,* Vol. 47 (1956), pp. 67–93; idem, "Furcht, wem Furcht gebührt. Zum profangriechischen Hintergrund von Rm 13, 7," *Zeitschrift für die neutestamentliche Wissenschaft,* Vol. 55 (1964), pp. 58–62; W. C. van Unnik, "Lob und Strafe durch die Obrigkeit. Hellenistisches zu Röm 13, 3–4," in *Jesus und Paulus: Festschrift für W. G. Kümmel zum 70. Geburtstag,* ed. by E. E. Ellis and E. Grässer (Göttingen: Vandenhoeck & Ruprecht, 1975), pp. 334–343.
47. Cf. Jewett, *Paul's Anthropological Terms,* p. 440.
48. Cranfield, *Romans,* p. 679.
49. The RSV translates *kai touto* (Rom. 13:14) with "Besides this," and the Käsemann commentary offers "Finally," both of which weaken the connection between vs. 8–10 and vs. 11–14. Cranfield is correct in insisting that the expression "is an idiom serving to introduce an additional circumstance heightening the force of what has been said" (Cranfield, *Romans,* p. 680).
50. Cf. Jewett, *Paul's Anthropological Terms,* p. 164.

Chapter V
GUIDELINES FOR TOLERANT CONGREGATIONS

1. Frederick W. Danker and Jan Schambach, *No Room in the Brotherhood: The Preus-Otten Purge of Missouri* (Clayton Publishing House, 1977), pp. 22–26.
2. Francis A. Schaeffer, *The Church Before the Watching World* (Inter-Varsity Press, 1971), p. 62.
3. Ibid., p. 81.
4. Ibid., p. 74.
5. Robert H. Schuller, *Your Church Has Real Possibilities!* (Regal Books, Divn. of G/L Publications, 1974), pp. 44f.
6. Ibid., p. 55.
7. Liberty Baptist College student handbook. As cited by Frances FitzGerald, "A Reporter at Large: A Disciplined, Charging Army," *The New Yorker,* Vol. 57, No. 13 (May 18, 1981), p. 74.
8. Jean Bodin, *Colloquium of the Seven About Secrets of the Sublime,* tr. from the Latin by M. L. D. Kuntz (Princeton University Press, 1975), p. 471.
9. James W. Fowler, *Stages of Faith: The Psychology of Human Development and the Quest for Meaning* (Harper & Row, Publish-

ers, 1981); and Jack Renard Pressau, *I'm Saved, You're Saved—Maybe* (John Knox Press, 1977).

10. Fowler, *Stages of Faith*, pp. 174–183.

11. Pressau, *I'm Saved*, pp. 51–53.

12. Ibid., pp. 16–17.

13. Käsemann, *Romans*, p. 353. Cf. note 38 of Chapter I, above.

14. Käsemann, *Romans*, p. 370.

15. Michel, *Römer*, p. 340.

16. Cranfield, *Romans*, p. 711.

17. Michel, *Römer*, p. 42.

18. Käsemann, *Romans*, p. 358.

19. John Murray (ed.), *The Epistle to the Romans* (2 vols., Wm. B. Eerdmans Publishing Co., 1960–66), Vol. II, p. 187.

20. Pressau, *I'm Saved*, p. 117.

21. Ibid., p. 125.

22. Martin Buber, *The Knowledge of Man: Selected Essays*, ed. by Maurice Friedman, tr. by Maurice Friedman and Ronald Gregor Smith (Harper & Row, Publishers, 1965), p. 60; as cited by Glenn Tinder, *Community: Reflections on a Tragic Ideal* (Louisiana State University Press, 1980), p. 84.

23. Barrett, *Romans*, p. 264; Käsemann, *Romans*, pp. 360f.

24. Käsemann, *Romans*, p. 361.

25. Douglas E. Wingeier, "Church Kitchen Theology," *The Circuit Rider*, Vol. 4, No. 2 (Feb. 1980), pp. 3–4.

26. Douglas E. Wingeier, *Working Out Your Own Beliefs* (Abingdon Press, 1980).

Conclusion

TOLERANCE AND MISSION

1. Dean M. Kelley, *Why Conservative Churches Are Growing: A Study in Sociology of Religion* (Harper & Row, Publishers, 1972), p. 83.

2. Ibid., p. 168.

3. Nils Alstrup Dahl, "The Missionary Theology in the Epistle to the Romans," in Dahl and Donahue, *Studies in Paul*, pp. 70–94, esp. p. 88: "The theology of Romans is closely tied to the Pauline mission with its historical and eschatological perspectives. . . . The task is rather to regain the unity of theology and evangelism, and of justification by faith and world mission."

4. Paul S. Minear, *The Obedience of Faith*, pp. 96f.

5. Ibid., p. 92.

6. Fowler, *Stages of Faith*, p. 293.

AUTHOR INDEX

SCRIPTURE INDEX

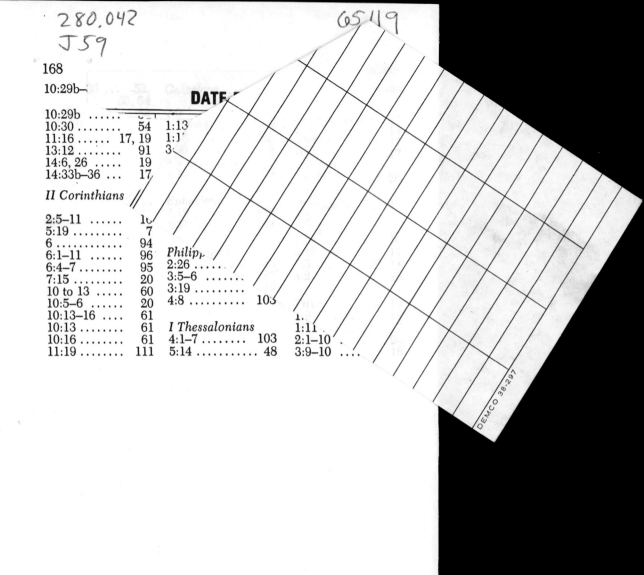